20107971

20107971

T 7849

Feb 06

IN
AMERICAN
HISTORY

THE BATTLE OF GETTYSBURG IN AMERICAN HISTORY

A E A

Ann Graham Gaines

Enslow Publishers, Inc.

40 Industrial Road   PO Box 38
Box 398   Aldershot
Berkeley Heights, NJ 07922   Hants GU12 6BP
USA   UK

http://www.enslow.com

Library of Congress Cataloging-in-Publication Data

Gaines, Ann.
    The Battle of Gettysburg in American history / Ann Graham Gaines.
      p. cm. — (In American history)
    Includes bibliographical references (p.) and index.
    Summary: Provides background on the bloodiest battle in the Civil War, a day-by-day account of the fighting, and a discussion of the battle's aftermath.
    ISBN 0-7660-1455-X
    1. Gettysburg (Pa.), Battle of, 1863—Juvenile literature. [1. Gettysburg (Pa.), Battle of, 1863. 2. United States—History—Civil War, 1861–1865—Campaigns.] I. Title. II. Series.
    E475.53 .G27   2001
    973.7'349—dc21

                          00-008973

Printed in the United States of America

10 9 8 7 6 5 4 3 2

To Our Readers: We have done our best to make sure all Internet addresses in this book were active and appropriate when we went to press. However, the author and the publisher have no control over and assume no liability for the material available on those Internet sites or on other Web sites they may link to. Any comments or suggestions can be sent by e-mail to comments@enslow.com or to the address on the back cover.

Illustration Credits: Alexander Gardner, *Photographic Sketch Book of the Civil War* (New York: Dover Publications, Inc., 1959), p. 39; Enslow Publishers, Inc., pp. 20, 32, 78; Frank Leslie, *The Soldier in Our Civil War*, (New York: Stanley-Bradley Publishing Co., 1894), pp. 87, 102; Kimberly Widenor, pp. 107, 110; Library of Congress, pp. 51, 58, 66, 83; National Archives, pp. 8, 22, 25, 28, 63, 64, 69, 73, 92; Reproduced from the *Dictionary of American Portraits*, Published by Dover Publications, Inc., in 1967, pp. 19, 37; Robert Underwood and Clarence Buel, *Battles and Leaders of the Civil War* (New York: Century, 1887), vol. 3, p. 50; Roy Meredith, *Mr. Lincoln's Camera Man*, 2nd Rev. ed. (New York: Dover Publications, Inc., 1974), p. 12.

Cover Illustration: Frank Leslie, *The Soldier in Our Civil War* (New York: Stanley-Bradley Publishing Co., 1894); National Archives.

★ CONTENTS ★

If someone had been standing on the bank of the Potomac River near Williamsport, Maryland, on June 15, 1863, he or she would have seen history march past.

A BATTLE FOUGHT BY SURPRISE

The local inhabitants noticed a few horsemen appearing from the woods on the south bank of the river in Virginia. After looking around, the riders spurred their horses on, splashing into the river at a shallow spot. They crossed to the north side, entering Maryland. Now they had left the Confederacy (the new nation Southern states had formed when they withdrew from the United States after disagreeing with Northerners over slavery and states' rights). They had entered Union territory.

Behind the first riders came a steady stream of horsemen. Eventually, two thousand men crossed the river and rode north. Uniforms and flags identified these men as Confederates. They were probably on a raid into Maryland and Pennsylvania—perhaps intending to steal supplies, local residents thought. All the locals could do was hope that these men would leave their property alone.

Perhaps an hour after the cavalry left, those still watching on the north bank saw a few men appear on foot from the woods on the other side of the river. These men plunged into the river just as the Confederate cavalry had done. Following them, column after column of infantry arrived, mixed with teams of horses pulling artillery guns and wagons. Again, the men crossed the river.

It was an impressive sight. Officers on horseback looked handsome in their neat gray uniforms. Some of the men carried flags that fluttered in the breeze. Brass bands played lively tunes and the men sang along. But the most striking thing was that all of the men on foot had taken off every scrap of their clothes. Soon the north bank was swarming with thousands of soldiers drying themselves off before getting dressed.

The seventy-five hundred men were Confederate soldiers. They belonged to a division of the Army of Northern Virginia commanded by General Robert Rodes. If they were here, the rest of the Confederate Army could not be far behind. The locals realized that fighting was coming to Maryland and Pennsylvania.

The soldiers did not put on neat gray uniforms. Instead, they wore a strange mix of clothes. Most men had a jacket or coat that was more or less gray. Shirts were whatever each individual had brought from home. A few men had proper gray uniform pants. Others wore the pants they had on when they enlisted. Many men wore blue trousers, originally part of a United States Army uniform. Everyone had something resembling a hat. Hundreds of men lacked shoes. During June and July, these men would have to march almost four hundred miles in their bare feet unless they could find new shoes.

While the Confederate troops marched through Maryland and Pennsylvania during the last half of June, they looked for supplies and food. Two years of war in Virginia had left the state barren. Pennsylvania, on the other hand, had not been touched. It seemed to be a land of plenty.

As the Army of Northern Virginia moved, it took all the cattle and horses it could find. When Confederate soldiers arrived in a new town, their commanding general would present town officials with a list of supplies the army needed. When General Jubal Early's division occupied York, Pennsylvania, the request was for enough food to feed eight thousand men for three days, all the hats and socks that were available, and two thousand pairs of shoes. Then, General Early asked that the shops be opened so his men could buy whatever else they needed.

On June 30, Confederate General Henry Heth's division arrived outside the small town of Gettysburg, Pennsylvania. Early's division had passed through a few days before. Heth sent one of his brigades to check the town for supplies, particularly shoes.

The brigade marched off toward town, but never made it there. Its commander, General James Johnston Pettigrew, stopped on top of a ridge outside of town. He could see Union cavalry ahead. He had been specifically told by Heth not to start a fight. So he turned his troops around and marched back to join the rest of the division.

Pettigrew reported what he had seen to General Heth. Heth, in turn, reported to his commander, General A. P. Hill. Hill thought about the situation briefly. He ordered Heth to take his entire division to Gettysburg to get rid of the Union troops there. Cavalry and the small group of militiamen they had also seen would not be able to stand up to infantry (foot soldiers with rifles) for long.

However, the Confederate Army's commander, General Robert E. Lee, had told his generals to avoid starting a major battle. At the moment, his Army of Northern Virginia was scattered too far apart. Lee wanted to engage his Union foe, but he did not think the time was right.

On the morning of July 1, General Heth had

General A. P. Hill was the one who accidentally started the Battle of Gettysburg by sending his troops to push Union soldiers out of town.

his division on the road to Gettysburg. A few miles outside of town, they ran into some Union cavalry. Obeying orders, his troops formed a line of battle and pressed forward. The Union cavalry fought stubbornly and with more strength than the Confederates had expected.

In time, the Confederate troops drove the Union cavalry back toward the town. The Confederates headed toward Gettysburg, too. But instead of the open road the Confederates had expected, they saw Union infantrymen rushing forward. The newcomers halted and opened fire. Despite Lee's instructions, A. P. Hill and his Confederate troops had started the Battle of Gettysburg, one of the bloodiest battles of the American Civil War.

2

BACKGROUND OF THE BATTLE OF GETTYSBURG

By the spring of 1863, the Civil War was two years old. Beginning in December 1860, Southern states had started to secede—or withdraw—from the United States. For years, Southerners had been discussing secession. They were alarmed by the increasing number of abolitionists in the North. Abolitionists wanted slavery to be outlawed. But the South's economy depended largely on slaves who grew cotton, tobacco, rice, and sugar cane for their masters. These crops demanded constant hard work in harsh conditions, work few free people would consent to do.

Many Southern politicians also supported secession. They believed the federal government violated states' rights. The Constitution said the states should remain sovereign, or self-governing. Southerners believed the government wanted to take away the states' ability to decide certain issues for themselves.

In November 1860, Abraham Lincoln, a Republican who stood firmly against the expansion of slavery into the American West, was elected president.

This caused Southerners to make their move. The first state to secede was South Carolina.

The South Secedes

Six other Southern states had seceded from the Union by February 1861. Along with South Carolina, they founded their own nation, the Confederate States of America, or the Confederacy. In the months that followed, the Confederacy established a government and prepared for the war all were expecting. In his inauguration speech, the new Confederate president, Jefferson Davis, appealed to the Union to leave the South alone.

United States President Abraham Lincoln told crowds that he considered it his duty to preserve the Union. In his inaugural address, he spoke to Southerners, "In your hands, my dissatisfied countrymen, and not in mine is the momentous issue of civil war. . . ."[1] He wanted the Southern states to come back to the United States. If they did not, the North would fight to force the South to return to the Union.

The Civil War Begins

On April 12, 1861, Confederate soldiers started the Civil War by firing on the Union soldiers who had refused to abandon Fort Sumter, a federal fort on an island in Charleston Harbor. Southerners believed that, after South Carolina seceded, Fort Sumter no longer sat on American soil. After Lincoln called on all the states, including those in the South, to supply troops

Abraham Lincoln's election as president of the United States proved to be the breaking point for many of the Southern states, which soon seceded from the Union.

SOURCE DOCUMENT

I THEREFORE CONSIDER THAT IN VIEW OF THE CONSTITUTION AND THE LAWS THAT THE UNION IS UNBROKEN, AND TO THE EXTENT OF MY ABILITY I SHALL TAKE CARE, AS THE CONSTITUTION ITSELF EXPRESSLY ENJOINS UPON ME, THAT THE LAWS OF THE UNION BE FAITHFULLY EXECUTED IN ALL THE STATES. . . . I TRUST THIS WILL NOT BE REGARDED AS A MENACE, BUT ONLY AS THE DECLARED PURPOSE OF THE UNION THAT IT WILL CONSTITUTIONALLY DEFEND AND MAINTAIN ITSELF.

IN DOING THIS, THERE NEEDS TO BE NO BLOODSHED OR VIOLENCE, AND THERE SHALL BE NONE UNLESS IT BE FORCED UPON THE NATIONAL AUTHORITY. THE POWER CONFIDED TO ME WILL BE USED TO HOLD, OCCUPY, AND POSSESS THE PROPERTY AND PLACES BELONGING TO THE GOVERNMENT . . . BUT BEYOND WHAT MIGHT BE NECESSARY FOR THESE OBJECTS, THERE WILL BE NO INVASION. . . .[2]

In his inaugural address, given on March 4, 1861, Lincoln explained that he did not believe the South could legally leave the Union and that he would simply be protecting public property by forcing the Southern states to return.

to put down what he called a rebellion, four more Southern states seceded. In the end, the Confederate States of America included eleven states: South Carolina, Mississippi, Florida, Alabama, Georgia, Louisiana, Texas, Virginia, Arkansas, Tennessee, and North Carolina. Four slave states—Maryland, Delaware, Kentucky, and Missouri—stayed in the Union, even though many of their people supported the Confederacy.

After Fort Sumter, both sides recruited thousands of new soldiers for their armies. The first large-scale engagement in the war took place near Manassas Junction, Virginia, in July 1861. Northerners later called this the First Battle of Bull Run. The Confederates, on the other hand, referred to it as the Battle of Manassas. (In general, the North named battles after nearby landmarks and the South named them after the nearest town.)

The Confederates won this battle, which turned out to be a bloodbath. Many people had come out from Washington, D.C., to watch, as if they were attending a picnic or concert. They fled for home horrified, leaving parasols and picnic baskets behind.

When the war began, many thought it would end quickly. Men eagerly signed up for the Union and Confederate armies. People on both sides believed that their cause was just.

At first, soldiers actually looked forward to battle, hoping to win glory. War, however, would take a terrible toll on both the North and the South. It cost a terrible number of lives. Society was disrupted in every state. War broke up families. Many women took on enormous new responsibilities.

In the first year, the Confederacy almost suffered disaster when Union troops came within five miles of its capital, Richmond, Virginia. But when Union General George B. McClellan held off taking the city while he waited for new troops to arrive, Robert E. Lee took control of the Confederate Army of

Northern Virginia. Under his command, the South suffered many casualties in the Seven Days' Battles, but scared McClellan, who ordered his army to retreat. Lee also won a victory at the Second Battle of Bull Run.

Meanwhile, fighting took place between Union and Confederate armies in the West. The Union's efforts there revolved around seizing control of the Mississippi River, which would cut the Confederacy in two and help the North win the war quickly.

The South Attacks the North

For more than a year, all battles in the Civil War were fought on Southern soil. For a long time, the Confederates focused on defending their homeland, rather than attacking the enemy. Then, in August 1862, Braxton Bragg led a Confederate army into Kentucky from Tennessee. The Confederates established a state government there to challenge the government that had stayed in the Union.

In September 1862, Lee and his Army of Northern Virginia invaded Maryland, another border state that had remained in the Union. By attacking the North, the South hoped to persuade the border states that had not seceded to consider doing so. They also hoped to gain European recognition, put pressure on Northern people to push for an end to the war, and relieve those living in the Upper South.

Union and Confederate soldiers fought the Battle of Antietam (which Southerners called the Battle of

Sharpsburg) in Maryland, on September 17, 1862. The day has been described as the bloodiest in the Civil War. Twenty-four thousand soldiers died or were wounded there. The Battle of Antietam did not end as a clear-cut victory for either side. Nevertheless, President Lincoln considered it a Union win when Lee's Confederate army retreated back across the Potomac River into Virginia.

Antietam represented the Confederacy's first major attempt to take the war to the North.[3] It also spurred Lincoln to issue the preliminary Emancipation Proclamation, which would free the slaves in Confederate states. At first, the North had not officially been fighting the Civil War to end slavery. The war was merely a fight to bring the South back to the Union. However, President Lincoln eventually decided that one of the goals of the war should be emancipation.

1863 Opens

The Union opened the year 1863 on a sour note. At Fredericksburg, Virginia, on December 11 to 13, 1862, Confederate soldiers had achieved a victory. Confederate General Robert E. Lee's Army of Northern Virginia defeated Union General Ambrose Burnside's larger force. The victory was not enough, however, for the Confederates to bring the war to a close.

The Union continued to succeed in the West. Union forces stretched across the northern Confederacy, from central Virginia through Tennessee to the Mississippi River into Arkansas, and across the southern

SOURCE DOCUMENT

. . . ON THE 1ST DAY OF JANUARY, A.D. 1863, ALL PERSONS HELD AS SLAVES WITHIN ANY STATE OR DESIGNATED PART OF A STATE THE PEOPLE WHEREOF SHALL THEN BE IN REBELLION AGAINST THE UNITED STATES SHALL BE THEN, THENCEFORWARD, AND FOREVER FREE; AND THE EXECUTIVE GOVERNMENT OF THE UNITED STATES, INCLUDING THE MILITARY AND NAVAL AUTHORITY THEREOF, WILL RECOGNIZE AND MAINTAIN THE FREEDOM OF SUCH PERSONS AND WILL DO NO ACT OR ACTS TO REPRESS SUCH PERSONS, OR ANY OF THEM, IN ANY EFFORTS THEY MAY MAKE FOR THEIR ACTUAL FREEDOM.[4]

After the Battle of Antietam, President Lincoln issued the preliminary Emancipation Proclamation. It warned Confederates that, on January 1, 1863, he would free all slaves in Confederate territory.

Confederacy from southern Virginia and eastern North Carolina, down along the south Atlantic Coast and west as far as Texas. A lack of European recognition and aid also continued to threaten the life of the new Confederate nation.

Lee Wants to Go North Again

In February 1863, Lee asked Jedediah Hotchkiss to make him a map showing the roads in Pennsylvania that led to Philadelphia. Later in the spring, Lee asked the Confederate government in Richmond to authorize repairs to the Virginia Central Railroad, which he hoped to use to transport supplies to the Maryland border. He also started to round up the wagons he would need.[5] He had decided he needed to take the war north again so that the Union could not use its soldiers to attack Richmond. But first, he would have to deal with the enemy troops already in Virginia.

Chancellorsville

The Battle of Chancellorsville, Virginia, took place from May 2 through May 4, 1863. The Union forces there were led by a new commander, General Joseph Hooker. He had been appointed major general of the Army of the Potomac in January 1863. The Union Army frequently changed generals during the Civil War because none seemed capable of bringing the war to a quick end. President Lincoln hoped to find a general who would quickly defeat the Confederates and bring the South back to the Union.

Despite the fact that Union soldiers outnumbered Confederates by two to one, Chancellorsville was a glorious victory for the Confederacy. Union casualties totaled seventeen thousand men; the Confederacy suffered thirteen thousand casualties. Confederates, however, did have one especially terrible loss in the battle. Popular and successful Confederate General Thomas "Stonewall" Jackson died soon after the battle, accidentally shot by his own men. The defeat forced the Union Army to retreat. When he read the telegram informing the War Department of General Hooker's defeat, President Lincoln wrung his hands and exclaimed, "My God! My God! What will the country say?"[6]

Vicksburg

In May 1863, soldiers of both armies stretched across the Confederacy. However, there were only three places where decisive action seemed likely. One was in east-central Virginia, where the Confederate Army of Northern Virginia faced the Union Army of the Potomac. Another likely place was in Tennessee, where the Confederate Army of Tennessee faced the Union Army of the Cumberland. The third place was in western Mississippi. President Abraham Lincoln realized the importance of the port of Vicksburg, Mississippi, on the Mississippi River. Unless the Union Army took Vicksburg, the Confederacy could continue to receive supplies and new troops. Vicksburg played an important role in the

General Joseph Hooker, often called "Fighting Joe" by his men, was chosen by President Lincoln to lead the Union Army of the Potomac in January 1863. He soon disappointed Lincoln, like his predecessors.

economy, too. Western planters shipped cotton from there. If the Union could take control of Vicksburg, it would cut the Confederacy in half. Without the Mississippi River as a supply route, the Confederate Army would be unable to continue fighting.

Union General Ulysses S. Grant commanded the Army of Tennessee. He started to ferry his troops across the Mississippi River on April 30, 1863. Grant

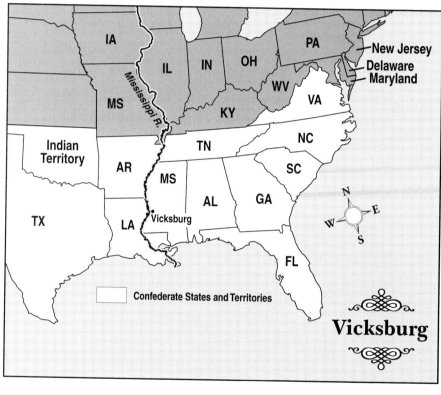

Vicksburg, Mississippi, located on the Mississippi River, was a strategic goal for the Union armies. If Union forces could take Vicksburg, they would control the Mississippi, thereby cutting the Confederacy in two and preventing it from moving supplies and messages quickly from one end of the country to another.

moved his troops across the river south of Vicksburg. Then he led them northeast. Finally, he had Vicksburg surrounded. He placed it under siege, surrounding it and preventing it from receiving or sending supplies and messages. The Confederacy faced a terrible crisis.

The Time Comes to Move North Again

From May 14 to 17, 1863, General Robert E. Lee met with Confederate President Jefferson Davis and his Cabinet in a series of strategy meetings in Richmond. Davis wanted Lee to take his Army of Northern Virginia west and fight Grant's Union Army at Vicksburg. By this time, Davis had long employed a defensive strategy. He concentrated on defending his country, often moving troops to protect key points in the Confederacy. Other military leaders, however, wanted to attack. They suggested that the Confederate Army mount an offensive in Tennessee.[7]

Lee, however, wanted to invade the North. He believed that, if the Confederates were to win the war, they had to act quickly. He hoped one great Confederate victory on Northern soil might lead the Union to surrender. At that time, there was a growing peace movement in the North. Many Northerners were tired of the hardships the war was causing. They thought the time had come to make peace with the South. Lee believed a Confederate victory would strengthen this movement and cause its members to pressure Union leaders to stop the war.

President Jefferson Davis trusted Robert E. Lee's judgment, and decided to allow Lee to attack the North.

A great victory on Union soil also seemed likely to bring international recognition for the Confederacy. If British Prime Minister Lord Palmerston and French Emperor Napoleon III decided to support the Confederate cause, they might lend the Confederacy money. They might even send troops. But it would take a great victory to convince these foreign powers that the Confederate cause was worthwhile.

Lee also thought that mounting an offensive against the Union would prevent its leaders from coordinating an attack of their own. They would have to start protecting their own cities and supply lines. The presence of Confederate forces on Northern soil might make the Army of the Potomac move troops away from both Richmond and Vicksburg. Fighting in the North would also mean that Lee could feed his army with Northern grain and livestock, easing the burden on the Southern states.

By the end of their meetings, Davis had agreed to Lee's proposal. On May 17, his Cabinet voted in favor of Lee's plan. They authorized what would be called the Gettysburg Campaign. They understood that Lee's army would be outmanned and outgunned. However, Lee's army had had fewer soldiers and weapons at both Fredericksburg and Chancellorsville, where the Confederates had won important victories. Although the Gettysburg Campaign involved great risk, it also held the promise of great reward.

3

THE GETTYSBURG CAMPAIGN BEGINS

In late May 1863, General Lee prepared to invade the North. His army then included about seventy-five thousand men. The army was supported by artillery, or cannons. Lee also had a first-rate cavalry.

At the Battle of Chancellorsville, Virginia, the Army of Northern Virginia's infantry had been divided into two main bodies called corps. After the death of General Stonewall Jackson, however, Lee divided his two infantry corps into three. General James Longstreet commanded I Corps. Lee gave command of what had been Stonewall Jackson's II Corps to Lieutenant General Richard S. Ewell.[1] The new III Corps he placed under the command of Lieutenant General A. P. Hill.

The Campaign Begins

Lee wanted Union forces to know he was on his way north. However, he hoped to hide his real objective. He hoped they would think the Confederates were headed for Washington, D.C., the capital of the United States.

"Stonewall" Jackson, who had earned his nickname for his bravery at the First Battle of Bull Run, was Lee's most trusted commander. His death left a crucial gap in Lee's chain of command.

Robert E. Lee wanted his Confederate army to reach Philadelphia and Baltimore. Then he could cut communication between Washington and the rest of the country. This would make it difficult for the United States government to function, and especially, to direct the Union Army. Invading these Northern cities would force Hooker to pursue Lee. This would let Lee choose where to fight, if he chose to fight at all.

Lee's army started its invasion of the Union on June 3, 1863.[2] The army had been in camps along the Rappahannock River in Virginia. First, it marched north to Culpeper Court House, in northern Virginia.

At that time, Lee's common soldiers had no idea where they were headed. General Richard S. Ewell's II Corps led the way. Longstreet's I Corps and Hill's III Corps followed. According to Lee's orders, the cavalry was to move independently of the rest of the army.

James Ewell Brown "J.E.B." Stuart led the Confederate cavalry. Thirty years old, Stuart had won glory when he staged a "Ride around McClellan" in June 1862. In three days, his cavalry rode one hundred fifty miles around George McClellan's Union forces. The entire time, Stuart's troops tormented their foe, burning Union camps, stealing Union horses, and cutting the telegraph lines that let Union generals communicate with Washington, D.C.[3] But his most important contributions came when he occupied ground that lay between the Army of Northern Virginia and the enemy. There, he could learn what the enemy was doing while preventing the Union from learning of his own army's movement. Aggressive reconnaissance—the missions of discovery Stuart undertook—was "his most significant contribution to Lee's army," according to historian Emory M. Thomas.[4]

At the beginning of the Gettysburg Campaign, J.E.B. Stuart and his cavalry troops were camped near Culpeper Court House at Brandy Station. Twice in early June, Stuart staged magnificent reviews, inviting audiences to watch his men practice their military maneuvers. Everybody was impressed. Ladies watching from grandstands fainted when long lines of horsemen, whooping and waving their swords in the air, rode full speed toward cannons firing blanks. Having arrived in time to see the second review, Lee wrote home to his wife that Stuart "was in all his glory."[5]

Brandy Station

Having gathered his men for those reviews, however, would prove unfortunate for Stuart. On the morning of June 9, 1863, Stuart's entire command, nearly ten thousand men, remained north of Culpeper Court House. Suddenly, Stuart was jolted awake by the sound of gunfire. From his camp on top of a hill, he watched as the slumbering camps below him dissolved into chaos. Confederate cavalrymen rushed from their tents, grabbed their weapons, and ran for their horses. Some managed to get dressed. A few headed off to fight in their underwear. As they poured eastward, they met Union cavalrymen headed west. Stuart leapt onto his horse, sent aides galloping to gather his other troops, and plunged down the hill into what would become known as the Battle of Brandy Station.

The commander of the Union's Army of the Potomac, General Joseph Hooker, had directed General Alfred Pleasonton and his cavalry to cross the Rappahannock River and smash the Confederate cavalry. If successful, Lee's plan to march north would be delayed. Any advance would be dangerous without cavalry to lead the way and protect the army.

Union General John Buford and his 1st Cavalry Division started the battle at 5:00 A.M. Splashing across the Rappahannock, his troops rushed westward toward Fleetwood Hill. A growing number of Confederates met him just before the hill. Men slashed with sabers or shot their enemies with pistols. By noon, both sides were exhausted. The fighting paused.

J.E.B. Stuart was one of the youngest generals of the Civil War, as well as one of the bravest.

Two other Union cavalry divisions crossed the river a few miles south of Buford. The 3rd Division followed a road to the west and out of the battle. The 2nd Division advanced a mile to the west and then turned north toward Fleetwood Hill. They met no one until they reached the top of the hill, behind the fighting between Buford's division and the Confederates.

Suddenly, Confederate troops appeared. A swirling fight broke out across the top of the hill. The Confederates were finally able to drive the Union troops from the hill. This brought an end to the fighting.

At 5:00 P.M., Pleasonton ordered his troops back across the Potomac. Historians recognize the Battle of Brandy Station as the largest cavalry battle ever to take place on the continent of North America.[6]

The Union had not done what it had set out to do. Stuart's division had been hurt, but not severely. The battle was a draw. But Brandy Station had one important result. Union cavalrymen found out that the Confederate cavalry was not invincible. One Union officer remembered realizing that the Confederate cavalry could not easily replace its horses when they became exhausted or hurt in battle.[7] The Union left the fight feeling better about themselves.

The Confederate cavalry did the opposite. Southern gentlemen prided themselves on their horsemanship. They believed Northern riders could never equal them. At Brandy Station, they clearly saw that the Union cavalry had become a dangerous force.

Earlier, these mounted Union soldiers had fought only with swords. They now carried rifles, too.

Stuart After Brandy Station

After Brandy Station, Stuart's men moved north. In northern Virginia, Confederate cavalry fought Union forces at Aldie on June 17, Middleburg on June 19, and Upperville on June 21. On June 22, Stuart was at Rector's Crossroads (about four miles west of Middleburg). From there, he wrote to Lee, asking what he should do next. Stuart wanted to keep harassing Hooker's army.

On June 23, Lee wrote back. He told Stuart he could follow Hooker only until the Union Army crossed the Potomac River. Then Stuart should ride into Pennsylvania and concentrate on keeping Lee informed of Union movements. He wanted Stuart to leave two of his brigades behind in the Blue Ridge Mountains. Lee left the route the other three brigades would take north to Pennsylvania up to Stuart.[8]

On June 25, Stuart began his ride to the Potomac. His cavalry crossed the river on June 28 in the middle of the night. At noon on June 28, he was in Rockville, Maryland. There, he cut the telegraph line and captured 125 wagons. The wagons slowed his progress from that point on. Only on July 1 did he begin to send scouts to look for Lee. Stuart fought at Carlisle that day. After a scout arrived with the information that Lee needed him, Stuart left Carlisle on July 2, around 1:00 A.M. He and his cavalry rode thirty-three miles to join the rest of Lee's army.

A New Union Commander

In early June, the Union's War Department learned that the Confederate Army was on the move. Union soldiers in hot air balloons had seen the Confederates marching north.

Learning this, President Lincoln immediately called a meeting with Union Major General Joseph Hooker, who commanded the Army of the Potomac. Lincoln asked Hooker to abandon his plans to attack Richmond. Instead, Hooker should pursue the Army

---

SOURCE DOCUMENT

I HAVE PLACED YOU AT THE HEAD OF THE ARMY OF THE POTOMAC. OF COURSE I HAVE DONE THIS UPON WHAT APPEAR TO ME TO BE SUFFICIENT REASONS. AND YET I THINK IT BEST FOR YOU TO KNOW THAT THERE ARE SOME THINGS IN REGARD TO WHICH, I AM NOT QUITE SATISFIED WITH YOU. . . . I HAVE HEARD, IN SUCH WAYS AS TO BELIEVE IT, OF YOUR RECENTLY SAYING THAT BOTH THE ARMY AND THE GOVERNMENT NEEDED A DICTATOR. OF COURSE IT WAS NOT *FOR* THIS, BUT IN SPITE OF IT, THAT I HAVE GIVEN YOU THE COMMAND. ONLY THOSE GENERALS WHO GAIN SUCCESSES, CAN SET UP DICTATORS. WHAT I NOW ASK OF YOU IS MILITARY SUCCESS, AND I WILL RISK THE DICTATORSHIP.[9]

President Lincoln quickly became unhappy with General Hooker's performance, writing him this letter just weeks after he took command of Union armies.

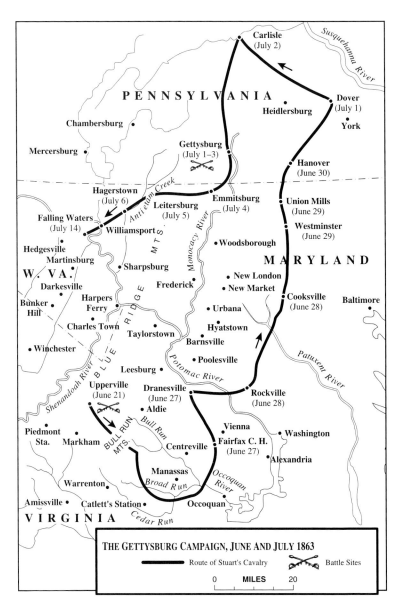

This map shows the places involved in Lee's Gettysburg Campaign, along with the route that J.E.B. Stuart used to reach Lee's Confederate Army. Historians have argued that, had Stuart used a shorter route, the Battle of Gettysburg might have turned out much differently.

of Northern Virginia. He wanted Hooker to face Lee in a decisive, head-to-head battle.

Hooker refused. He and Lincoln argued. Finally, Hooker became so frustrated that he asked to step down from his command. Lincoln gladly accepted his resignation. George Meade assumed command of the Army of the Potomac on June 27, 1863.

The Union Chases the Confederates

Lee's army had started to cross the Potomac River into Maryland in the middle of June. All were across by the end of the month. By then, the Union Army had begun to move, following the Confederates. When Lee found out that the Northern army was close by, he was alarmed. He was accustomed to indecision and slowness on the part of Union commanders.

By June 24, even Confederate privates (the lowest rank of soldiers) knew their destination was Pennsylvania. The citizens of Pennsylvania had also learned that the Confederates were coming. Notices in the newspaper called for new recruits to join the Army of the Potomac. The men of Maryland and Pennsylvania would soon need to defend their land and their families.

Confederates on Union Soil

Confederate soldiers had had good morale from the beginning of the Gettysburg Campaign. The march northward was not easy. They had to travel a great distance, day after day. Some of the land they crossed was mountainous, which made marching hard. In

Confederate territory, they saw depressing, war-torn land. Near Tappahannock, Virginia, a Confederate wrote in his diary that he saw "[scarce] a farmyard that is not stained by human blood. Scarce a field unpolluted by the enemy's touch. The fences are burned, the meadows trampled down, the cattle all gone and the harvests unharvested; proud homesteads in ruins. . . ."[10]

The temperature rose as high as 95°F by afternoon. Soldiers sweated and kicked up clouds of dust, which clung to their clothes, hair, and faces. Some fell behind, suffering from sunstroke.

But the soldiers had confidence in Robert E. Lee. They thought about their recent string of successes. In Union territory, Confederate morale ran even higher than before. Lee's soldiers had been lacking supplies. Many wore rags. Some men marched barefoot or in makeshift shoes. As they marched, their officers seized supplies. The Confederate soldiers became better fed and more comfortable as they went along.

Lee had ordered his troops not to steal. He wanted his officers to pay for any goods—food, fodder, and horses—they took. Soldiers, however, seem to have stolen anyway. General Ewell had to warn his men in mid-June that "this plundering must be repressed [stopped] or our discipline is gone."[11]

At least some Confederate soldiers saw plundering as their right. "The wrath of southern vengeance will be wrecked upon the pennsilvanians & all property belonging to the abolition horde which we may cross. We will try & pay them for what they have been doing to the innocent & helpless in our good southern land," William H. Routt wrote in a letter.[12] Another soldier remembered that his comrades "took everything they could lay their hands on. . . ."[13]

This plundering had grave consequences for the Confederates. When fighting in Virginia, they had fought to defend their homes and families. They were focused on the fight. This helped them endure great hardship. "On the raid into Pennsylvania, foraging and plundering dulled their edge," historian Joseph Glatthaar concluded.[14] Officers gave in to their men's desires. Discipline broke down.

The Union Army Moves

After the Battle of Chancellorsville, soldiers in the Union Army of the Potomac suffered from low morale. Sergeant Horace Smith recorded in his diary, "The roads and fields are filled with troops going back to their old camps, but a more disheartened set of fellows I never saw. All because we were ordered to retreat."[15] The soldiers had lost confidence in their leaders.

By mid-June, the Union Army of the Potomac began to move. Major General Carl Schurz remembered that the Union soldiers "were ready and eager to march and fight."[16] Like the Confederate soldiers, Union troops had a hard march but experienced a surge in morale after they crossed the border into Maryland. In northern Virginia, in the words of Lieutenant Albert Wallber, they had seen "nothing but those melancholy pine forests, barren, impoverished fields . . . and old dilapidated homes."[17] In Maryland, by contrast, they saw well-tended gardens and fields. Their mood became even better once they left Maryland, a slave state where many citizens supported the Confederacy. In Pennsylvania, they enjoyed support from the public. Crowds gathered to cheer them as they marched by. They also had a renewed dedication to the fight. Now they were fighting to drive invaders from their own land.

On June 28, General George Meade took control of the Army of the Potomac. Most common soldiers considered this good news. By June 29, the Union troops expected a major battle soon.

One of Meade's first actions was to send Major General John Buford and his cavalry to find the Army of Northern Virginia. Just behind Buford, Meade sent Major General John Reynolds and one third of the Army of the Potomac's infantry. Meade had to defend Washington, Philadelphia, and Baltimore. He could not let Lee's army, piece by piece, attack these cities. Instead, Hooker wanted to force Lee's army to come together and fight.

The First Confederates Reach Gettysburg

On June 26, Confederate General Jubal Early's division arrived in Gettysburg. Gettysburg was located just inside Pennsylvania, seven miles from Maryland. Surrounded by many other small towns, it sat 62 miles north of Washington, D.C., and 110 miles west

George Meade (seen here) replaced Joseph Hooker as commander of the Union Army just before the Battle of Gettysburg took place.

of Philadelphia. Fertile farmland surrounded the town. The landscape was rolling, with few trees. A series of ridges, or long, low rises, about two miles in length, ran north to south, west of town. Just south of town sat Cemetery Hill and Culp's Hill. Two more big hills, Little Round Top and Big Round Top, were located farther south, at the end of Cemetery Ridge.

Gettysburg had a population of about twenty-four hundred. As the seat of Adams County, it was an important commercial center. Eleven roads converged in the town. It had a courthouse, seven churches, nine lawyers' officers, taverns, hotels, a prison, a Lutheran seminary, and was home to Pennsylvania College.[18] It also had an iron works, a foundry, a stove factory, a brickyard, and a tannery.[19]

Legends later said Early sent word to Lee that he had seen a shoe factory in Gettysburg. Confederate soldiers desperately needed shoes. According to these legends, Early thought his fellow commanders would want to come and seize such a valuable supply. Today, however, many historians deny the shoe factory story. The 1860 census indicated there was no shoe factory in Gettysburg.[20] However, Gettysburg did have many other kinds of supplies that the Confederate Army needed.

By now, the Confederate Army was widely spread out. Ewell's corps was north and east of Gettysburg. Hill and Longstreet were west of Gettysburg, in Chambersburg. Historians believe Lee still thought the Union Army was south of the Potomac River, since he received no word otherwise from Stuart.

On June 28, however, Lee learned from a scout named Henry T. Harrison that the entire Union Army of the Potomac had crossed the Potomac.[21] In reaction to the news, on June 29, Lee sent out messengers with orders for all his forces to assemble in the vicinity of Cashtown and Gettysburg.[22] He feared that, if he did not assemble his whole army, the Confederates might encounter the Union Army piece by piece and end up destroyed. Even as Lee issued this order, Union forces, unknown to Lee, were heading toward Emmitsburg, another small town close to Gettysburg.

A First Glimpse of the Union Foe

On June 29, Heth's division led the Confederate Army toward Gettysburg, marching from Chambersburg to Cashtown, eight miles west of Gettysburg. The first Confederate infantry brigade arrived on June 30.

A view of the town of Gettysburg taken from Cemetery Ridge, after Union soldiers made camp.

James Johnston Pettigrew marched his men toward the town early in the morning, under orders to go there for supplies. As he approached, Pettigrew spied Union cavalry. He ordered his troops to withdraw. By 11:00 A.M., Buford's Union cavalry rode into town.

Later, Pettigrew told Heth about the cavalry he had seen. He repeated his story to Hill, too. Hill's scouts had said that the Union Army's tents remained up many miles away. Hill believed Pettigrew had seen just a small detachment of Union soldiers. He did not believe there were others in the area. Pettigrew tried to make his point again.

Hoping Hill would be persuaded if someone else told him that a large Union cavalry was nearby,

Pettigrew asked Captain Louis Young to tell Hill what he had seen. Young told Hill that he fully believed he had seen seasoned cavalrymen—not members of a small local militia, organized to defend the town.

Hill still thought Pettigrew and Young were mistaken. He could not believe that the entire Army of the Potomac was on the move. Pettigrew later wrote that Heth then brought up his desire to march into Gettysburg the next morning. Contributing to the idea that the Confederate Army went to Gettysburg for shoes, Pettigrew quoted Heth as saying, "If there is no objection, I will take my division to-morrow and go to Gettysburg and get those shoes." Hill replied, "None in the world."[23]

The Union Cavalry

In the meantime, Union cavalry General John Buford was beginning to realize that he was probably very close to Lee's Confederate Army. Looking over the surrounding countryside from Cemetery Hill, he had seen men in gray uniforms on the road. At first, he thought they were a small raiding party, hunting for food. When he counted six company flags, he knew he was looking at a large number of men. He sent word back to his commanders. On June 30, Union Army chief commander Meade issued orders to his I Corps to march to Gettysburg on July 1. By that point, Buford had ordered his men to dig in.

The Town of Gettysburg Prepares

Residents of Gettysburg had feared invasion for a long time when Lee headed north in the summer of 1863. Gettysburg schoolteacher Sallie Myers wrote,

> It was early in June that we had the first reports the rebels were coming. Naturally, the people of the town became terribly excited. . . . Bankers sent their money away. Merchants sent their goods to Philadelphia and other places for safety. Day after day the people did little but stand along the streets in groups and talk. Whenever someone heard a new report all flocked to him. The suspense was dreadful. . . .[24]

By late June, local residents realized that Lee's army would very likely march through their area soon. Farmers drove their animals to safety. Some residents fled town. On June 26, the 26th Pennsylvania Emergency Volunteer Infantry (a local militia that included only men from Gettysburg) came upon Confederate soldiers. They fled, because they lacked enough men to fight.[25]

When Early rode through town on June 26, he stopped his men in its main square. He then ordered townspeople to send for Gettysburg's officials. From David Kendlehart, the president of the town council, Early demanded money. He also wanted seven thousand pounds of bacon, twelve hundred pounds of sugar, sixty barrels of flour, six hundred pounds of coffee, one thousand pairs of shoes, and five hundred hats.[26] Kendlehart replied that the town did not have such great quantities available. The best he could do was ask local merchants to open their stores so that the Confederate Army could take what it could use.

On June 28, residents saw Union cavalry pass through their town. Local people lined the streets to give their soldiers food. On June 30, people living in Gettysburg could see Confederate pickets on Seminary Ridge. When Union cavalry General Buford arrived in town, he and his men received an enthusiastic welcome. Residents invited Union soldiers to dinner.

On the Eve of Battle

As the sun set on June 30, 1863, two huge armies had come very close to each other. The Army of the Potomac stretched from five to twenty-five miles from Gettysburg. The Army of Northern Virginia was spread out in a similar fashion. Together, these armies included about one hundred sixty thousand men.[27] The Army of the Potomac, commanded by General George Meade, had eighty-five thousand to ninety thousand men. Lee's army had about seventy-seven thousand.

Today, looking back, we know that June 30 was the eve of the Battle of Gettysburg. Neither Meade nor Lee—nor their men—however, knew what was about to take place. The Battle of Gettysburg would be, for everyone involved, a surprise.

Neither Confederate General Lee nor Union General Meade planned to fight the Battle of Gettysburg. In fact, Lee had expressly said he did not want to fight the enemy until his army had reunited. Confederate and Union soldiers met at Gettysburg by chance. It was what military historians call a "meeting engagement," or an

THE FIRST DAY: JULY 1, 1863

unplanned, accidental encounter. Meade was just as surprised as Lee had been to encounter a large number of enemy troops.[1]

A Chance Meeting Becomes a Battle

The Battle of Gettysburg began early in the morning on July 1, 1863. It did not follow a planned course. Commanders often had to decide what to do next based on guesses—guesses concerning the strength of the enemy or how nearby land lay, for example. Generals often stated that one of their biggest problems during the Civil War was that battlefields were terribly confusing. It was hard to see the big picture— to understand the movement of the enemy as a whole.

This stemmed, in part, from the fact that officers could only see what was happening immediately around them. Battles sometimes covered a great deal of territory. Also, smoke often rose above a battlefield, making it hard to see more than a few yards away.

The Battle of Gettysburg, like many other Civil War engagements, was basically a fight between infantries. Military officials on both sides generally believed that the best tactic to adopt in battle was to make a mass infantry charge against the opposing army's weakest point.[2]

From the First Battle of Bull Run, a pattern was set. Two armies approached each other. Their commanders each formed lines of infantry. One line of soldiers simply marched toward the other, knowing they would soon meet a volley of ammunition. The soldiers carried rifles loaded with soft lead bullets. After every shot, most rifles had to be reloaded. If lines got close enough, infantrymen attached bayonets to their guns, which they used like spears to stab their enemy. Battles ended when one side withdrew.

The soldiers who fought in the Civil War lived through horrifying experiences. Over and over again, they had to show great courage when they took to the battlefield, knowing that they would soon be part of a bloodbath. Thousands died on the field. Those who were wounded often suffered extreme pain. The weapons of the day inflicted horrible wounds. Those who were shot in a limb almost always had to undergo amputation. Lying in makeshift, understaffed hospitals, many died of infection and disease.

The life of a Civil War soldier, whether he fought for the North or the South, was hard off the battlefield as well. Members of both armies endured long marches on a regular basis. In camp, they tried to enjoy themselves, telling stories, playing cards, or singing. But much of the time, soldiers experienced great boredom, as they waited for fighting to take place.

The Confederates Meet the Union Cavalry

On the morning of July 1, General A. P. Hill felt sick. He stayed behind in Cashtown, but he sent Major General Heth to Gettysburg. Hill was under orders from Lee to avoid fighting until Lee's entire army had gathered in the same place.[3] Officially, Hill sent Heth to Gettysburg to look for provisions, including, perhaps, the legendary shoes. Later, critics accused Hill of sending Heth toward Gettysburg knowing he would find Union cavalry there and that fighting would ensue.[4] Today, some scholars believe Hill thought Heth would meet little Union resistance there. Others believe Heth's men went prepared to fight.[5]

Inside the Town of Gettysburg

When residents of Gettysburg got up on the morning of July 1, they could only have imagined the terror the day would hold. They had seen soldiers from both armies over the past few days. On June 29, Sallie Myers had written in her diary, "we may expect a battle both near and soon."[6] Looking back, local resident Harriet Bayly wrote, "The whole air seemed charged with conditions which go before a storm. . . ."[7]

Nevertheless, as the day began, most people in Gettysburg simply went about their business as usual. Merchants opened their stores. College classes met in the morning, but soon the sound of gunfire made it impossible to pay attention. At that point, some residents of Gettysburg ventured out to see what was going on. Three boys climbed a hill north of town. They began to feel fear when "we noticed up the road, coming over the nearest hill, great masses of troops. . . ."[8]

The First Encounter

Around 8:00 A.M., Confederate General Henry Heth and his division approached Gettysburg from the west on a road called Chambersburg Pike. Reaching a crest of land called Herr Ridge, Heth surveyed the scene. Deciding they would meet little Union resistance, Heth ordered two brigades, led by Brigadier General James J. Archer and Brigadier General Joseph Davis, to advance and occupy Gettysburg.

On their way, those two Confederate infantry brigades ran into Union cavalry. Union General Buford had seen the Confederate soldiers who came toward Gettysburg the day before. One of his subordinates had commented that he thought they dared not return and that, if they did, he could beat them off easily. Buford disagreed. "No, you won't," he said. "They will attack you in the morning and they will come booming—skirmishers three deep. You will have to fight like the devil until supports arrive."[9] To prepare, Buford had formed his own battle line. He had ordered his men off their horses along Seminary Ridge about a mile west of Gettysburg. It was these soldiers whom the Confederates first encountered. Marching up Seminary Ridge, they found themselves suddenly under attack.

Heavy fighting occurred. Both sides sent for reinforcements. Finally, the Confederates forced the Union soldiers to retreat. At that point, the Confederates could have abandoned the idea of continuing on into Gettysburg. There were supplies in other towns. But General Hill decided to continue the fight.

A New Round of Fighting

Even as Buford and his cavalry retreated, a Union corps arrived, under the command of John F. Reynolds, who ordered five thousand of his men into the fight. He sent the rest to occupy Gettysburg. Under orders from Reynolds, two Union brigades relieved Buford and occupied McPherson's Ridge, another crest just west of town.

Reynolds watched his men's movements from inside some woods. Seeing the Confederates, he sent a message to Union Corps XI and III to advance to Gettysburg. He told Meade they would meet the enemy there in force. "I will fight him inch by inch, and if driven into town I will barricade the streets and hold him back as long as possible," he informed Meade.[10]

Reynolds never had a chance to act on his resolution. Before the fighting really began, he was killed by a Confederate sharpshooter. He died instantly from a single shot to the head.

In the meantime, the Confederates had started to move forward toward McPherson's Ridge. Southern Generals James Archer and Joseph Davis ordered their men to attack again. Caught between two groups of Union soldiers, Archer and many of his men were captured.[11] Archer was the first high-ranking officer from Lee's army ever taken prisoner.[12] Those of his men who escaped death or capture had to retreat.

– At first, Davis's soldiers had more success. They inflicted heavy casualties on the Union troops they met. But when three Confederate regiments suddenly found themselves under attack, they sought shelter in an unfinished railroad cut. This trench had steep walls twenty feet high. Union soldiers soon appeared above the cut. The Confederates had to drop their weapons and allow themselves to be taken prisoner. Altogether, half of Davis's brigade was captured in the cut. Those who escaped retreated to Herr Ridge, where they found the remnants of Archer's brigade.

The Locals Realize the Fighting Is Real

That morning, local boys watched the fighting from the cupola, or tower, of one of the local seminary's buildings. Other citizens watched from Seminary Ridge or from rooftops in town. When Union reinforcements headed toward the fighting, girls turned out to cheer them on, wave their handkerchiefs, and shout words of encouragement.

Soon, however, local residents realized how much destruction they were about to face. Much of the fighting took place on farmland. The landmarks where fighting took place, such as McPherson's Ridge and Culp's Hill, bore the names of local families.

Some families witnessed fighting up close. Amelia Harmon and her aunt were in their house near Seminary Ridge around 9:00 A.M., when they heard a cannon nearby. Running upstairs, they threw open a window. From there, they could see that a field between their woods and their barn was filled with crouching Confederate soldiers, stealthily moving forward. As Union cavalrymen approached them, the Confederates would stand and fire at them. Amelia saw a Union officer's horse shot right under her window.[13]

Other residents ventured out of their houses, hoping to get out of the way of the fighting. Ten-year-old Sadie Bushman was heading across a field, toward her grandparents' house, when a shell whizzed right by, brushing her skirt. A Union Army surgeon appeared, seemingly out of nowhere. He took her to a sheltered place where he had set up a tent and was tending wounded soldiers. There, despite her age, he put Sadie to work. Sadie took care of a wounded man, giving him a drink of water, while his leg was amputated.[14]

Confederates under Colonel John Brockenbrough attack Union troops at the McPherson farmhouse on July 1, 1863. Much of the fighting took place on the property of local Gettysburg residents.

By late morning, the town and countryside had become quiet. Shops had shut down. Residents of Gettysburg had hurried home. As noon approached, town constable John Burns decided he had to join the fight on the side of the Union. He was then nearly seventy years old. As a younger man, he had fought in the War of 1812 and the Mexican War. He had tried to enlist in the Union Army when the war first broke out, but was told he was too old. Still wanting to serve his country, he drove an army wagon for a time, but then returned home. When the Battle of Gettysburg began, however, Burns took out the gun he had used fifty

John Burns, seen here at the age of seventy-two, was a civilian hero, wounded at the Battle of Gettysburg.

years earlier in the War of 1812 and marched off
toward the sound of fighting. At McPherson's farm, he
joined the 150th Pennsylvania regiment. That day, he
was wounded three separate times. But he survived the
battle.[15]

The Battle Starts Yet Again

A pause in the fighting followed the retreat of Archer
and Davis's Confederate brigades. By this time, reinforcements had arrived for both sides. Fighting broke
out again in the afternoon when Confederate Major
General Robert Rodes, part of General Ewell's command, ordered two brigades, led by Alfred Iverson and
Edward A. O'Neal, to advance. Rodes had intended to
have them attack the Union brigade commanded by
Henry Baxter at the same time. But Iverson held back,
waiting for his side's artillery to hurt Baxter. This left
O'Neal's brigade out alone in front.

O'Neal had chosen not to accompany his
brigade—he stayed behind with the reserve regiment.[16]
Marching forward, his 1,688 men reached a stone wall.
From behind, Union soldiers opened fire. They immediately killed or wounded almost seven hundred
Confederates. The rest of O'Neal's brigade had no
choice but to turn and run for their lives.

Iverson finally sent his own brigade down the
western slope of Oak Ridge. Their march ended when
Union soldiers mowed them down with bullets. One
surviving member of the 12th North Carolina remembered that, until that moment, he had not seen a single

Union soldier.[17] Facing gunfire at point-blank range, the Confederates fell quickly. Afterward, seventy-nine North Carolinians lay dead in a straight line.[18] When the smoke cleared, more than 70 percent of Iverson's command had died, been wounded, or were captured. Like O'Neal, Iverson had watched his men die from a distance. "Unwarned, unled as a brigade, we went to our doom. Deep and long must the desolate homes and orphan children of North Carolina rue the rashness of that hour," a survivor wrote.[19]

This was just one dramatic moment in a long afternoon of fighting that ultimately ended in the Confederates' favor. Eventually, Confederate Generals Robert Rodes and Jubal Early forced the Union soldiers to retreat into and through Gettysburg. Farmer Nathaniel Lightner later described watching Union soldiers dodging to get out of their way: "A mad rush of . . . troops, wagons, and ambulances followed, filling up streets, orchards, fields, and every place."[20]

Leadership

In the meantime, Union General Oliver O. Howard sent one of his brigades south to Cemetery Hill. He ordered the troops to wait there. They were to stand by as reserves.

Confederate General Hill arrived around noon. He and Lee had heard the battle from Cashtown. Lee arrived about 2:30 P.M. Almost immediately, he set up headquarters in the home of Mary Thompson, near the crest of Seminary Ridge. There, Lee met with his staff

SOURCE DOCUMENT

EVERY SIZE AND FORM OF SHELL KNOWN TO BRITISH AND TO AMERICAN GUNNERY SHRIEKED, MOANED, WHIRLED, WHISTLED, AND WRATHFULLY FLUTTERED OVER OUR GROUND. . . . THROUGH THE MIDST OF THE STORM OF SCREAMING AND EXPLODING SHELLS AN AMBULANCE, DRIVEN BY ITS FRENZIED CONDUCTOR AT FULL SPEED, PRESENTED TO ALL OF US THE MARVELLOUS SPECTACLE OF A HORSE GOING RAPIDLY ON THREE LEGS. A HINDER ONE HAD BEEN SHOT OFF. . . .[21]

Samuel Wilkenson wrote this account of the Battle of Gettysburg as he sat beside the body of his son, Bayard, who had been killed in the fighting.

and ate. He slept, however, in his own tent across Chambersburg Pike.

As commander of the Confederate Army of Northern Virginia, Lee assumed responsibility for the battle. He could have ordered a retreat. Instead, he decided to escalate the battle.

Apparently, Lee considered the situation fortunate. He ordered Hill to join the battle and continue the assault Heth's men had begun in the morning. Fierce and bloody fighting followed.

Hill sent out J. Johnston Pettigrew's Confederate brigade of more than twenty-five hundred men to attack Solomon Meredith's Union brigade, which still occupied McPherson's Ridge. Although both sides fought hard, Pettigrew's brigade finally forced Meredith to retreat toward Seminary Ridge.

Both sides had suffered devastating losses. In one half hour of fighting, the Union's Iron Brigade suffered 1,153 casualties. In one Confederate company of ninety-one men, every single soldier fell on the field, wounded or dead.[22]

As Heth's men were getting tired, Confederate General W. Dorsey Pender entered the battle. Three of his brigades ran up Seminary Ridge, where Union soldiers had begun to build fortifications. The Union troops held off the Confederates for only a few minutes. Soon the Union I Corps was retreating toward town and Cemetery Ridge. At the same time, the Union XI Corps was retreating toward Cemetery Hill.

The Townspeople Hide

By this time, the town of Gettysburg was a scene of mass confusion. When the Union soldiers started to retreat through town, officers warned the people of Gettysburg to hide. Anna Garlach remembered looking out her window on a street crowded with Union soldiers. As they passed her house, they yelled to the townspeople to go to their cellars.

Albertus McCreary, who lived in a stone house, recalled that several families crowded into his home. He first realized how grim the situation was when, from his basement, he heard someone say, "Shoot that fellow going over the fence." And that was just the beginning. Soon he recalled hearing "one continuous racket" of shooting.[23]

Chasing their enemy, Confederates captured fourteen hundred members of the Union XI Corps.[24] Union General Alexander Schimmelfennig escaped capture by hiding in a ditch.[25] Residents hid others. Beating a hasty retreat just ahead of Confederate troops, several Union soldiers hid in the basement of the Sheads residence. A Confederate sergeant ran in and cornered Union Colonel Charles Wheelock. The Confederate demanded the Union colonel's sword. Wheelock claimed he had already given it up. Actually, Carrie Sheads had hidden it in the folds of her dress. After the battle, Wheelock escaped from his Confederate captors and returned to the Sheads house to claim his sword. Another Union soldier captured at the Sheads house later returned, too. He married Louise Sheads, Carrie's sister.[26]

Fighting Ends for the Day

As evening approached, Confederate troops occupied the town of Gettysburg. That night, they demanded food from residents. They also searched homes for hidden Union soldiers.

Some townspeople came out of hiding. Many went to work in the makeshift hospitals that had sprung up all over town. Union and Confederate wounded filled churches, stores, and the courthouse.

The Confederates had won the first day of battle. However, they had suffered terrible casualties. Many soldiers on both sides had died. Others had been wounded. They still lacked supplies. Like the Union soldiers, the Confederates were also very tired. They had been on the march for close to a month.

The Union had suffered a defeat that day. Eighteen thousand Union soldiers had been involved in the fighting. Nine thousand had been injured or killed. Nevertheless, the Union's situation began to improve overnight. The division on Cemetery Hill had been busy all afternoon, fortifying its position.

Ewell Stays Put

For a time, it seemed that fighting might resume late in the afternoon of July 1. Confederate Generals A. P. Hill and Robert E. Lee stood together on Seminary Ridge around 4:30 P.M. Hill said he would fight no more that day. He thought the enemy was "entirely routed."[27] His own men were exhausted. Lee apparently agreed that Hill's men could not do any more at the time.

Ewell, in the meantime, sent Lee a message. Ewell said that, if Hill would agree to join in, he, Rodes, and Early would launch a new attack. According to Captain Walter H. Taylor, Lee replied, saying that, since the enemy was fleeing, Ewell alone could take Cemetery Hill. Lee and Ewell, however, both later said that Lee had told Ewell to secure the heights south of town "if practicable."[28]

Lee had meant for Ewell to try to establish a Confederate position there. Ewell misunderstood. He thought he was being given a choice as to whether to continue to fight. In the end, he decided not to attack

These are just a few of the Confederate dead who fell on one day of the Battle of Gettysburg.

Cemetery Hill and Culp's Hill that afternoon. He thought that he could not push the Union soldiers off the hills. To capture Cemetery Hill, Ewell could not simply continue what he had been doing. He would have to make a new assault, after gathering troops who had scattered.

Ewell's failure to act would become one of biggest controversies of the entire war. Confederate Major General Isaac Ridgeway Trimble recorded in his diary that Ewell had made *"a radical error."*[29] A junior officer wrote soon after the battle that he believed just five hundred Confederate soldiers could have taken the hills, saying, "The simplest soldier in the ranks felt it."[30] Five years later, while reminiscing, Lee himself stated that Ewell fought in an "imperfect, halting way."[31] Many modern scholars have accused Ewell of being indecisive. Some, however, have pointed out that Ewell did not know how weak the Union defense actually was. He had no information about how many troops he faced.[32]

At the end of the day, Ewell remained where he had been since the afternoon. Lee finally went to see him, hoping to spur him to action. Then Lee realized that, because of Ewell's delay, the opportunity to attack was gone. The Army of Northern Virginia could do no more until the next day.

The Union Reforms

As night fell, the Confederates could count the day as a huge victory. In addition, General James Longstreet had arrived. New men would be available to fight the next day.

But the Union Army of the Potomac was in the process of assuming a great defensive position, reforming its lines on Cemetery Hill. Drawn on a map, the Union arrangement was shaped like a fishhook. Union soldiers were working to increase the strength of their position by using logs, branches, and stones to form barricades. Many would sleep just one hour during the night. In the morning, they would be following the orders of their new commander, Union General George Meade, who had just arrived.

5

THE SECOND DAY: JULY 2, 1863

After the fighting ended on July 1, the Confederate Army of Northern Virginia and the Union Army of the Potomac continued to gather. Union Army General George Meade's forces on Cemetery Hill and along Cemetery Ridge were arranged in the shape of a fishhook, placed upside down with the hook to the right. Meade ordered his forces to fortify their positions. The Union was preparing for the assault he expected the Confederates to make in the morning.

Plans for Another Day of Fighting

Confederate General Robert E. Lee had a tough decision to make. Several choices faced him. He could retreat. He could move his army away from Gettysburg and prepare to fight elsewhere. Lee could do as the Union was doing—assume a defensive position and wait for the enemy to attack. Or he could launch his own attack.

Lee decided to attack. He might have decided differently had Stuart been there, but the cavalry was still miles away. Lee had just learned that Stuart and his forces were near Carlisle and could not arrive before the next day. Lee also rejected the idea of taking a defensive position. He believed his army lacked the supplies needed to simply wait for a Union attack. His men were living off the land. They had to keep moving if they were to survive.

Lee decided to strike at both ends of Meade's line. He ordered General Richard Ewell to assault Culp's Hill, where the Union's right flank sat. He ordered General James Longstreet to attack the Union left flank from the west. Longstreet protested. He did not believe the Army of Northern Virginia should attack that day. But Lee prevailed.[1]

Lee also decided that General A. P. Hill should wait for orders in the center of the line. Then, as circumstances dictated, Hill could attack the middle of the Union forces or send men to fight on either end. No one should begin to fight, Lee said, until Longstreet got into position.

A Quiet Morning

There was no fighting on the morning of July 2. The Union Army continued to fortify its position. Meade wanted his men to form a solid line. His XII Corps held Culp's Hill. What remained of the Union I Corps occupied the land between Culp's Hill and Cemetery Hill. Oliver O. Howard's XI Corps was positioned on Cemetery Hill. Winfield Scott Hancock's II Corps covered Cemetery Ridge, just south of Cemetery Hill.

Meade wanted Union Major General Daniel E. Sickles's divisions also placed on Cemetery Ridge, at its end, to anchor the Union left.

Sickles, however, decided that Cemetery Ridge was not high enough. He moved his corps a mile from where Meade wanted him, into what was known as the Peach Orchard. This created a gap in the Union line, with the Union left flank undefended. Learning of Sickles's action, Meade ordered Sickles to return to Cemetery Ridge, but there was no time for him to do so. By this time, the Army of Northern Virginia was in position. Spirits ran high among the soldiers in gray.

Longstreet Gets His Troops Into Position

According to Lee's plan, Confederate General James Longstreet was supposed to attack the Union's left flank. It had taken him all day to get his men into position. Longstreet had available two divisions—twelve thousand and fourteen thousand men. (One division— General George Pickett's—had not yet arrived.)

General Longstreet's soldiers may have felt confident, but they had made a long trek under a brutally hot sun. They had arrived at the fight already tired. Robert E. Lee, back at headquarters, had been waiting hours for the news that Longstreet was in position. One of his staff members later remembered Lee's asking, "in a tone of uneasiness, 'what can detain Longstreet? He ought to be in position now.'"[2]

General James Longstreet was often called General Lee's "Warhorse."

Fighting in the Peach Orchard

Around 4:00 P.M., Longstreet finally launched his attack. What would follow was "one of the war's most desperate engagements," according to historian Robert K. Krick.[3] Longstreet used artillery to attack Union General Daniel Sickles's troops in the Peach Orchard. Longstreet also sent John Bell Hood's and then Lafayette McLaws's divisions to fight.

Despite their fatigue, Longstreet's men made a "furious" attack.[4] Sickles's Union soldiers came under attack from three sides and suffered terrible casualties. Sickles himself had his left leg shattered by a cannonball in the fighting.

Devil's Den

When it became evident that Sickles's Union troops were in trouble, Union General George Meade ordered General Winfield Scott Hancock to send a division to assist Sickles. Those Union soldiers who could still stand deserted the Wheatfield and the Peach Orchard. They would try to hold a new position, in what they called Devil's Den—a terribly rocky and hilly area.

There, Union soldiers from Pennsylvania, New York, Maine, and Indiana fought Confederate soldiers from Texas and Arkansas. Just beyond Devil's Den, there was wild fighting in the area of a creek known as Plum Run. Later, participants in this part of the fighting called the area the Valley of Death. A Texan later recalled: "The balls are whizzing so thick that it looks like a man could hold out a hat and catch it full."[5]

This Confederate sharpshooter was killed during the fighting at Devil's Den.

The Round Tops

In the meantime, the Confederate 15th Alabama had scrambled up a nearby hill called Big Round Top. From it, their colonel, William C. Oates, could get a good view of the surrounding terrain. He immediately realized that, if the Confederates could also take nearby Little Round Top, they would assume a position from which they could attack the Union Army with artillery. They might even be able to smash the entire Union line. When Oates inspected Little Round Top from Big Round Top, however, there were only a few Union soldiers there. This would soon change.

Union General Meade had sent General Gouverneur K. Warren to Little Round Top to assess the situation. Warren also realized the importance of the position. Seeing Confederates advance out of Devil's Den, he rode for reinforcements. Fortunately for the Union, he soon found a brigade under the command of George Sykes. Sykes sent four Union regiments, including the 20th Maine, commanded by Colonel Joshua Chamberlain, up Little Round Top. At the same time, Warren had men haul field artillery up the hill.

Fierce fighting broke out. Many regiments fought desperately. One especially dramatic moment took place between regiments from Alabama and Maine. The Confederates charged the Union line over and over. Union Captain Howard Prince remembered watching the enemy head at him: "Again and again this mad rush repeated, each time to be beaten off by the

Some of the most terrible fighting of the Battle of Gettysburg took place when Union and Confederate forces clashed as they tried to occupy Little Round Top, seen here as it looked soon after the battle.

ever-thinning line that desperately clung to its ledge of rock."[6] The 20th Maine used twenty thousand rounds of ammunition. As the Union soldiers ran out of bullets, they charged with bayonets. By the end of the charge, one third of the 20th Maine's soldiers were killed or wounded.

The situation was even worse for the 15th Alabama, of which one half were killed, wounded, or captured. Colonel William Oates later recalled, "My dead and wounded were nearly as great in number as those still on duty. They literally covered the ground. The blood stood in puddles in some places on the rocks; the ground was soaked with the blood of as brave men as ever fell on the red field of battle."[7]

Cemetery Ridge

Once the Union Army finally secured the Round Tops, the fighting continued between the hills and the top of Cemetery Ridge. For a time, there was a huge gap in the Union infantry in that area, although the Union artillery continued to fire. At one point, 262 members of the 1st Minnesota, bayonets fixed, ran down Cemetery Ridge to face sixteen hundred Confederates. They caught their enemy by surprise. Many Confederates died. Those who did not were captured. The Southerners fell back.

Finally, the Union line closed back up, but at great expense. Only forty-seven of the Minnesota men remained standing five minutes after their attack began. All the rest had died or been wounded. Not one had been captured. The Minnesota 1st sustained the highest percentage of casualties of any Union regiment during the war.[8]

On the Union Right Flank

In the meantime, the Confederates had also attacked the right flank of the Union Army. At about 4:00 P.M., Confederate General Richard Ewell's corps launched an artillery attack on Culp's Hill. At 7:00 P.M., Ewell sent the division commanded by General Edward Johnson up Culp's Hill to attack the Union fortifications. They fought valiantly, launching four attacks, one after the other. But they were unable to break through.

As darkness fell, reinforcements arrived to help secure the Union position on top of Culp's Hill. Another four brigades came to join Johnson's three. The Confederates continued to hold the lower hill.

Confederate General Jubal Early also directed fighting that evening, just north of Culp's Hill. The Union prevailed on that side of Culp's Hill, but the Confederates had success on Cemetery Hill, where several Louisiana regiments overran the Union XI Corps artillery. Only after dark did Union reserves arrive. Then, the soldiers from Louisiana were driven back to their own lines.

The End of the Day

Fighting went on that day until dark and beyond. After hours in the field, great portions of both armies were in disarray. When the fighting finally stopped, both sides were exhausted. The Union Army had shown tremendous staying-power. It had held Culp's Hill and Little Round Top and beaten Confederate General Hill's division back from Cemetery Ridge. Early's attack had also been repulsed.

Still, Union losses during the day were terrible. Casualties numbered around ninety-five hundred men.[9] Union commander Meade had lost about twenty thousand men in the two days of fighting.

The Confederates had also fought with fury. However, they had not won a victory and had suffered serious losses. Their casualties probably numbered around sixty-five hundred men.[10] Some historians believed Lee had not yet achieved his usual level of success because he had changed his battle strategy. In the past, Confederate victories had come from exploiting Union weak spots. On July 2, however, the Confederates had deliberately attacked the Union where it was strong.

Both Union and Confederate dead are seen in the photograph taken after the battle by Timothy O'Sullivan.

In Town

July 2 had been a difficult day for the people of Gettysburg, as well as those who were fighting. During the day, Union troops had occupied some sections of town. The Confederates occupied a larger part of town. Sharpshooters had taken over some houses. While John Rupp hid in his cellar, Union soldiers occupied his front porch and Confederates took over rooms at the back. Confederate soldiers had taken over the McCreary family's house. Union sharpshooters shot one of the soldiers through a window while he was standing in a room upstairs.[11]

All day, many townspeople stayed in the hiding places they had used the day before. Others came out of their cellars, but stayed inside their houses. Looking out his window, Charles McCurdy could see a Lutheran church that had been turned into a hospital. He wrote that its yard was filled with arms and legs as surgeons worked around the clock, performing amputations.[12]

Some residents of Gettysburg did go out. Sarah Broadhead recorded in her diary that her husband went out of their house to their garden, where, despite bullets flying through the air, he picked their entire bean crop. He did not want to leave a single bean for a Confederate soldier to eat.[13]

Leander Warren remembered his parents arguing. His father wanted the family to leave town, but his mother was in the process of baking bread she intended to take to wounded Union soldiers. She refused to go.

Harriet Bayly lived three miles north of Gettysburg. From her window, she could see where fighting had taken place the day before. Wounded men still lay on the battlefield, so she packed a basket with bread, butter, wine, bandages, and pins. Then, she and her niece mounted their blind horse and set off to help the wounded Union soldiers. In a nearby valley, she found men suffering extremely not only from their injuries, but from a lack of food and water and the hot July sun. Her niece gave out bread and wine, while Harriet Bayly bandaged wounds.

What Next?

At the end of the day, Union General Meade called his senior commanders together for a strategy meeting. He asked the generals whether they wanted to stay or retreat. Many historians believe that he wanted to bow out of the fight. But his commanders decided to stay and prepare to fight again the next day.

Confederate General Lee also spent the night thinking about what to do next. He felt frustrated. His army was still winning. But he had hoped that his victory would be more decisive and the losses not so high. At this point, he again considered his options. Then, like Meade, he made plans for a third day of fighting.

Lee hoped to be able to crack through the Union center the next day. That is where he thought the Union's Army of the Potomac had weakened. Lee had new forces to fight with—General George Pickett's division had arrived.

So had the Confederate cavalry. During the afternoon of July 2, Stuart had finally arrived. Accounts vary widely as to Lee's reception of him. Stuart had been out of touch with Lee for days. He had disobeyed Lee's orders to keep him informed of Union troop movements, choosing instead to harass the Union Army. This had hurt Lee immensely, causing parts of his army to stumble across the enemy.

One of Stuart's men, Major Henry McClellan, reported that the meeting between Lee and Stuart was painful. He said Lee became red in the face when he saw Stuart. He lifted his hand as though he wanted to hit Stuart and said to him, "I have not heard a word from you for days, and you the eyes and ears of my army." Stuart replied by pointing out that he had captured 125 Union wagons and the horses to pull them. Lee snapped back that he did not need them now. His anger then seemed to fade. McClellan described him as saying they should not discuss the matter further. What he needed was for Stuart to join in the fight.[14] Later, in his own report on the battle, Lee said nothing more about Stuart's late arrival than that "The movements of the army preceding the battle of Gettysburg had been much embarrassed by the absence of the cavalry."[15] Perhaps now that Lee had his cavalry to work with the battle could be won.

Overnight

That night, neither side slept much. The Union troops carried with them rations to eat. Many of the Confederates had none. Everyone was terribly thirsty. It was hot even at night, and no one could find much water.

Stretcher patrols from both armies worked through the night. They removed wounded men from the battlefields. Some individual soldiers also went back to places where they had fought, looking for friends and comrades. In most of both armies' companies, the soldiers all came from a single town or county. The men had often known each other for years. To locate

Almost every available building became a makeshift hospital. In this photograph, an army doctor performs an amputation on a soldier badly wounded in the fighting.

wounded men, soldiers followed the sounds of wails and groans. The wounded were then carried to makeshift hospitals. Practically every local building was used to house wounded and dying men.

Those who did stay in the armies' camps also got little sleep. The Union men who occupied the top of Culp's Hill and the Confederate men who occupied the bottom kept one eye open. They knew fighting would break out just as soon as there was enough light to see. A Union soldier remembered that, even though he was exhausted, he could do no more than doze:

> As we lay on our backs courting sleep, we could at any time see the skies crossed with a network of the fiery traces of shells going and coming, like shooting stars, between the artillery of both sides. Shortly afterwards it became quiet, [terrifyingly] so considering the storm we all knew had been brewing for the morrow.[16]

Everyone realized they would see more horror the next day.

THE THIRD DAY: JULY 3, 1863

When the third day of the battle, July 3, dawned, Union General George Meade's plan was to hold his positions on Cemetery Ridge and Culp's Hill. Confederate General Robert E. Lee, on the other hand, planned a new attack. The night before, he had drawn up his first plan. It called for Richard Ewell and James Longstreet to attack. Lee wanted to strike both flanks of the Union Army of the Potomac at the same time.

The next morning, on July 3, just after the sun rose, Lee mounted his faithful horse Traveller and rode to the far right flank of his army. There, Lafayette McLaws's and John Bell Hood's divisions, which made up Longstreet's command, had spent the night. It was there that Lee discovered he would have to change his plans.

As he spoke with Longstreet, they could already hear artillery fire. Union troops on the Round Tops posed a threat to Longstreet and his men that Lee had not expected. The night before, Lee had instructed Longstreet to attack the Union line just in front of him in the morning. But when Lee talked to Longstreet, he discovered that Longstreet had instead ordered his men to undertake a complicated flanking maneuver that would bring them around the Round Tops. Longstreet wanted his corps to attack the Union from the rear rather than from the front.

Lee immediately canceled Longstreet's orders. Lee had changed his mind. He decided not to strike his enemy's flanks, but to concentrate on attacking the Union center. The main thrust of the attack would involve between ten and fifteen thousand men.[1] Lee would use General George Pickett's division, which was rested and ready to fight. To back up Pickett, Lee would use infantry from both Hill's and Longstreet's corps.

A secondary attack would come from Ewell's corps from the north and from Stuart's cavalry, which was supposed to go around the Union's right flank and attack from the rear. Union General Meade actually expected the Confederates to launch their main assault at his center. Later, one general remembered that Meade had said Lee would try to attack the center because he had already failed to take out both flanks.

Fighting Begins

Preparations had begun deep in the night. On both sides, generals moved their men into new lines. After marching all day and into the night, at 2:00 A.M., Confederate artillerymen put cannons into position. Lee wanted the guns to be aimed at the center of the

SOURCE DOCUMENT

FROM THE SUDDENNESS OF THE REPULSE OF THE LAST CHARGE ON JULY 3RD, IT BECAME NECESSARY FOR GENERAL MEADE TO DECIDE AT ONCE WHAT TO DO. I RODE UP TO HIM, AND, AFTER CONGRATULATING HIM ON THE SPLENDID CONDUCT OF THE ARMY, I SAID: "GENERAL, I WILL GIVE YOU HALF AN HOUR TO SHOW YOURSELF A GREAT GENERAL. ORDER THE ARMY TO ADVANCE, WHILE I WILL TAKE THE CAVALRY, GET IN LEE'S REAR, AND WE WILL FINISH THE CAMPAIGN IN A WEEK." HE REPLIED: "HOW DO YOU KNOW LEE WILL NOT ATTACK ME AGAIN; WE HAVE DONE WELL ENOUGH."[2]

Union General Alfred Pleasonton later gave this report of his activity during the Battle of Gettysburg.

Union line. Rolling their guns through the Peach Orchard and Wheatfield, where Sickles's men had fought the previous afternoon, the Confederates had no choice but to roll over dead soldiers. There were no clear paths available.

After completing their task, the Confederate artillerymen finally had a chance to think of their own thirst and hunger. For two days, they had eaten almost nothing. The Army of Northern Virginia lacked food for both its men and its animals. Until they reached Gettysburg, these soldiers had been living off the land and what they could buy or take from locals. That night, the men assigned to the cannons suffered from such terrible hunger that they went through the pockets of their dead enemies, looking for any kind of food.

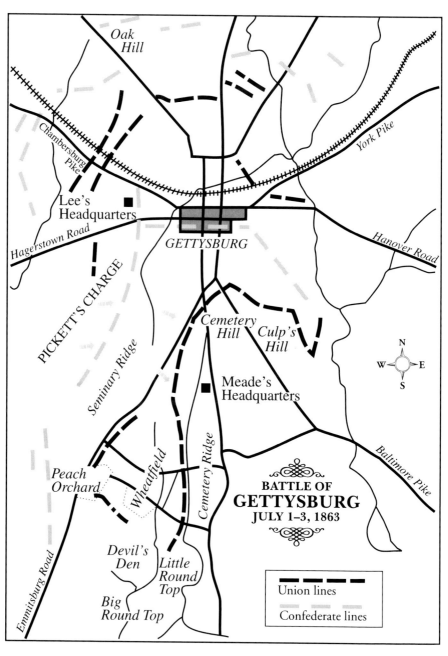

This map shows how the Union and Confederate forces were
spread out over the fields of battle at Gettysburg.

Ewell's Attack

All night long, the Union soldiers on Culp's Hill worked on building fences out of rocks and logs. Ewell's Confederates were awake long before dawn. They had spent the night halfway up Culp's Hill.

By 4:00 A.M., fighting broke out. Overnight, the Union commander at the top of the hill had sent half his corps away, to strengthen the Union left. But they returned in the morning. Reinforcements stood ready.

The Stonewall Brigade, the group formerly led by Confederate General Stonewall Jackson, which had already distinguished itself in battle, led four other brigades. They ran straight up Culp's Hill. The Union counterattacked from above, stopping the Confederate advance. But the Confederates regrouped. In all, the Confederates made four tries at taking Culp's Hill. By 11:00 A.M., all had been driven back. In the attempt, hundreds had died. Lee's plan for a coordinated attack seemed to be falling apart.

Stuart

Confederate General J.E.B. Stuart and his cavalrymen also failed in their mission. Lee had ordered Stuart to get behind the Union lines and attack from the rear. But Union cavalry had stopped him. Union cavalry on a road outside town had watched the Confederates advance through woods. The Union men had to admit that the Confederate men made an awesome sight. "They [approached] with well-aligned fronts and steady reins. Their polished saber-blades dazzled in the sun," one Union soldier later wrote.[3]

But then the Union troops rushed forward to meet Stuart's column. Racing toward one another, soldiers crashed, creating a sound one participant compared to "falling timber."[4] Many horses fell on their riders, crushing them. From horseback and on foot, the cavalries ended up fighting hand-to-hand.

In retrospect, it seems Stuart should have won this engagement. He had six thousand horsemen. The Union had only three thousand. Had he succeeded, Stuart could have gone on to break the Union battle-line and perhaps save the day for the Confederates. Earlier, Stuart might have done so. But by this time, Stuart was too tired. He suffered from what Lee biographer Douglas Southall Freeman called the "fog of war," losing his ability to think clearly.[5]

A Death in Town

That same morning, the only civilian killed during the Battle of Gettysburg died. Jennie Wade was twenty years old. When the battle broke out, her sister, Georgiana Wade McClellan, had just given birth to a baby boy. Jennie went to stay with Georgiana in her house on the south side of town.

On the morning of July 3, most townspeople were still hiding. They left their houses only during lulls in the fighting. Jennie Wade had left her sister's house several times over the past two days to carry water to wounded soldiers near the house. That morning, she had stayed inside to bake bread in her sister's kitchen. Confederate snipers were firing at Union soldiers outside. Suddenly, a bullet went through two of the house's wooden doors and struck Jennie in the back. She died instantly.[6]

The Artillery Barrage

Preparing for the charge Lee had planned, the Confederates opened a huge artillery attack at 1:00 P.M. Lee hoped this attack would crush the Union's front line, thus clearing the way for a charge. The Confederates had lined up 176 huge guns along Seminary Ridge, in a line almost a mile long. Witnesses would later disagree as to exactly how long they continued firing. One Union soldier said it went on for ten minutes. Many more thought it lasted up to three hours.[7] This difference in opinion shows how difficult it was for soldiers to know what was going on in battle. For some, time seemed to slow to a standstill. For others, everything seemed to occur in a rush.

The fierce fighting of the morning had occurred on Culp's Hill. Most of the Union soldiers on Cemetery Ridge had been relaxing—writing letters, playing cards, telling stories—when the cannons began firing. Suddenly, shells started to explode all around them. On Cemetery Hill, a single shell instantly killed twenty-seven Union soldiers.

The attack won little for the Confederates. The shells failed to take out much of the Union's front line, although they did create chaos in the back. Historians often say the Confederate cannons were aimed too high. Some historians, however, suggest that the problem was not with aim. Instead, shells manufactured at different arsenals exploded at different rates. The Confederate artillerymen at Gettysburg were used to using shells produced by the arsenal at Richmond. They knew exactly how to make them explode where and when they wanted. But there had recently been an explosion at the Richmond arsenal. It no longer produced shells. The Confederate artillerymen did not realize that the shells they were now using had fuses that burned more slowly—and so they burst behind the Union lines.[8] The Union did not have such a problem. Union shells firing back hit many Confederate infantrymen who were waiting for orders to attack.

Pickett Prepares

Pickett's men had marched all day on July 2 to get near Gettysburg. That night, they slept in a patch of woods along Chambersburg Pike, three miles away from town. At 3:00 A.M., their bugler woke them. Boys and men lit fires and made coffee. Before dawn, they were lined up, ready to march again.

Pickett led a line of men a mile long. To this day, it remains unclear why Confederate General James Longstreet had not ordered Pickett's troops to march all night and reach him by daybreak. As things went, Pickett was not on the battlefield until 9:00 A.M.[9] His troops were not ready to fight until late morning.

In the afternoon, Lee launched his final assault, which went down in history as Pickett's Charge. Lee made plans for fifteen thousand Confederate soldiers to charge. Lee hoped this would cause the Union line to crumble in the middle. If Lee could break up the Union Army, it would be easier to defeat.

In reality, Lee did not have fifteen thousand soldiers available. The exact number of Confederate infantrymen is not known. Some estimate thirteen thousand, others ten thousand five hundred.[10] Such confusion is hardly surprising. Historian Carol Reardon pointed out that, while Pickett's Charge is one of the best-known events in American history, very little is actually known firsthand about what happened there. Participants saw only the portion of the battle that took place near them. They had no way of seeing all of what was going on. Lee presumably had the best vantage point.

General George Edward Pickett was appointed to be commander of the famous failed Confederate charge on July 3, 1863.

He watched the entire charge from a command post behind his lines. But in the aftermath, he never wrote more than a few pages about all of what happened at Gettysburg, much less about the specific event of Pickett's Charge.

Around 2:30 P.M., the Union forces cut back their artillery attack. The Confederate soldiers waiting to make their assault watched the smoke clear and saw horses and soldiers pulling cannons back from the ridge. Confederate Colonel E. Porter Alexander sent a scribbled message from Lee to Pickett, saying the time had come to move.

Pickett went to Longstreet for approval. His men had been lined up for hours, waiting for this moment. According to one story, General Longstreet could not bear to give the command to begin the charge. He believed the troops had no chance of success. Rather than use words, at 3:00 P.M., he simply bowed his head to indicate that the time had come. Pickett moved to the front of his line. Encouraging his men, he shouted, "Charge the enemy and remember old Virginia!"[11]

Pickett's Charge

The first troops to emerge from Seminary Ridge's tree-line seem to have been those commanded by Johnson Pettigrew. Those commanded by Pickett and Isaac Trimble emerged probably just seconds later. More than ten thousand men raced across a mile of open ground. They all wanted to make it up Cemetery Ridge, where they could engage the Union in close combat. They aimed for a tiny grove of trees at the Union center.

Union soldiers immediately spotted the advance. First, they saw the Confederate flags. Then, they saw a mass of men marching straight toward them. The Union side had been lined up for hours, ready to meet the Confederate charge. Close to six thousand infantrymen, five hundred gunners, and twenty-three cannons formed a line three fifths of a mile long. They waited impatiently for the command to fire at the charging Confederates.

On and on, the Confederate soldiers marched. As they came within a thousand feet of the Union line, cannons suddenly opened fire from Union positions on Cemetery Ridge and Little Round Top. Some of the cannons fired exploding shells. Union Major Charles Peyton remembered "their fearful effect, sometimes as many as ten men being killed and wounded by the bursting of a single shell."[12]

– When the line reached close range, other cannons fired canister shot—cans filled with musket balls. These acted like giant shotguns. The Union artillery killed many Confederate soldiers immediately. Years later, members of the 8th Ohio still vividly remembered watching Confederate body parts—arms, hands, and heads—as well as blankets, guns, and knapsacks suddenly fly into the air.[13]

The Confederate artillery did not return fire. They had used up their ammunition. They could not back up their marching comrades. Yet, even in the face of cannons, the Confederate line continued to march. For a moment, the Confederates paused. When they got near Emmitsburg Road, they had to march through a dip that offered them a little bit of cover. There, the Confederate regiments halted for a moment to close the gaps the dead and wounded had left. They reformed their lines and started to march again. As soon as they crossed the road, the Union infantrymen opened fire on them.

As they neared the ridge, a Confederate lieutenant cried out, "Home, boys, home! Remember, home is over beyond those hills!"[14] As they climbed, they faced a terrifying number of weapons. In one place, Confederate Colonel Birkett D. Fry's brigade suddenly found itself facing seventeen hundred muskets and thirteen cannons. Confederates died or fell wounded in huge numbers. Many of those who survived could stand the withering fire for only a short time. They retreated or surrendered.

Only a few hundred Confederates reached the top of Cemetery Ridge. Confederates crossed the Union line just once, in a place participants called the Angle. It was a spot where a stone wall changed direction. There, Confederate General Lewis Armistead and three hundred fifty infantrymen climbed over the wall. It seemed for a time that the Confederates would actually get through the Union line. But then Union troops opened fire. Armistead and many of his companions died. There was a second, brief penetration, but

This image of Pickett's Charge was based on a sketch made during the battle by A. Berghaus.

nowhere else did the Confederates seriously threaten the Union line.

The End

By 4:00 P.M., Pickett's Charge was over. It had been a disaster. The Confederate survivors who had not given themselves up to Union troops had turned around. They were trying to make it back alive.

Lee, who had watched the charge from behind, rode out when he saw his men drifting back. At first, he tried to rally them, to convince them to go back and fight some more. Wanting to show them that he did not blame them for turning back, he told them, "It [the disaster] was all my fault."[15] At first, he begged them to go back and try to save the day. Then he realized that there could be no second charge.

Nevertheless, Lee expected the battle to continue. He hoped the Union troops would come out from behind the fortifications they had built and fight on the field. But Meade's troops did not do so. Meade's subordinate General Henry J. Hunt later explained,

> A prompt counter-charge after combat between two small bodies of men is one thing; the change from the defensive to the offensive of an army is quite another. To have made such a change to the offensive, on the assumption that Lee had made no provision against a reverse, would have been rash in the extreme.[16]

The Cost of the Charge

On July 3, sixty-five hundred Confederates died or were wounded. Fifteen regimental commanders had taken part in Pickett's Charge. Every single one had fallen. One entire company had been killed or wounded. Thousands more threw down their weapons and gave themselves up as prisoners. The Union Army had suffered just fifteen hundred casualties.

Finally, Lee ordered a retreat. The exhausted soldiers on both sides then faced a terrible task. They had to search for wounded, who were loaded into wagons and carried to makeshift hospitals. They also identified and buried dead comrades. These tasks took Union soldiers days. The Confederates had to leave many members of their army behind, unburied.

In town, the people of Gettysburg remained in hiding for hours. Sarah Broadhead wrote in her diary on the afternoon of July 3 that they could not tell who had won the battle.[17] Gettysburg resident Henry Minnigh had been away from home for months, fighting in the Union Army. His regiment had participated in the Battle of Gettysburg. After Pickett's Charge failed, Minnigh decided to leave his unit and see what was going on at home. At his parents' house, he found his entire family still hiding in the cellar. They were "a perfect image of dejection and despondency," he said. They had spent two days in the tiny, underground room lit by a single candle.[18] They expressed great joy when he told them of the day's outcome.

By evening, townspeople began to move about. That night, thousands of Confederate soldiers marched through town, heading for the South. A Mr. Benner remembered hearing Confederate wagons rattling through the streets all night.[19] The residents of Gettysburg felt tremendous relief. They would witness no more fighting.

AFTERMATH

On the night of July 3, 1863, General Robert E. Lee began to pull back his Confederate forces. He ordered General Richard Ewell's men away from Cemetery Hill. He had General James Longstreet's men abandon their positions in front of the Round Tops. He had as many Confederate wounded as possible loaded onto wagons, which headed first west and then south for home.

The Armies Wait

On July 4, it rained all day. What was left of the Confederate Army of Northern Virginia remained near the previous day's battlefield. At that time, it appeared as if the battle might break out yet again. All day, everyone in the area listened for the sound of gunfire. But Union General Meade never took the offensive.

Meade was a cautious man.[1] To attack seemed too risky to him. Meade did send out scouting parties to locate the Confederate soldiers and see if they were getting ready for battle. But he never ordered an attack. Instead, he had his men spend the day burying the Union dead and marking graves with temporary wooden headboards. At the same time, the Union soldiers searched for usable equipment abandoned by Confederates on the field.

Toward the end of the day, Lee ordered his Confederate troops to begin the march home. As the sun went down, they set out. On the night of July 4, the Union Army did strike at the Confederates. Soldiers commanded by Union Major General William H. French rode to Falling Waters, Virginia (now in West Virginia), where they destroyed a bridge Lee's men could easily have used on their flight toward home.

That night, Union cavalrymen also harassed the drivers of some of Ewell's wagons. On July 5, J.E.B. Stuart rode at the head of his cavalry into Emmitsburg at dawn, where they captured some Union soldiers. They also seized much-needed medical supplies.

What Gettysburg Cost the Armies

In leaving the field, Lee had acknowledged that the Battle of Gettysburg was over. Both sides had suffered terrible losses there. At the time, neither commander knew exactly what the battle had cost. Some soldiers were still separated from their regiments. It would take days, even weeks, for some of the wounded to die. It would take even longer to find out how many of the survivors would be able to fight again.

To this day, historians argue over the exact number of casualties at Gettysburg. What is clear is that both armies left the field smaller by the tens of thousands. According to the *Official Records of the Union and Confederate Armies,* the Army of Northern Virginia

These Confederate prisoners remained in Union custody after the Battle of Gettysburg.

had 2,592 soldiers dead, 12,706 wounded, and 5,150 captured or missing, making its total casualties 20,448.[2] The same source says the Union casualties totaled 23,049. Some historians believe the losses must have been even higher. Although Union losses at Gettysburg were higher than Confederate losses, they represented a smaller percentage of the total army. The Union Army could also replace men more easily, because the Union had a bigger population.

The Cost for the Town

Residents of the town of Gettysburg had suffered greatly during the battle. Confederate and Union troops had filled the streets. Later, residents told about harrowing escapes.

The town's population included 190 African Americans. As a group, they had become terrified when they learned that the Confederates were marching toward Gettysburg. Fearing being forced into slavery, many had fled their homes. One African-American woman had been captured by Confederates, but escaped and hid in a belfry for two days.

Many of the white residents of town hid during the battle. Sarah Broadhead remembered having hidden for three days in cellars. Other residents had hidden Union soldiers. Catherine Foster had hidden a Union soldier from Confederate searchers.[3] The Forney family had disguised a Union soldier so he could escape. Confederate patrols had searched residents' houses, looking for food, supplies, and Union soldiers. Residents had seen thousands of soldiers dead, dying, and wounded. They had had to bury one of their own, Jennie Wade. During the battle and for days afterward, schoolteacher Salome Myers and many other women tended wounded soldiers from both sides.[4]

As a whole, the town had supported the Union cause before and during the battle. Four out of every five residents had been born in Pennsylvania. When the war broke out, many of its men had joined the Union Army. Women had done their part by forming a ladies' relief society and contributing time and money to the war effort. Nevertheless, during and after the battle, they fed, lodged, and cared for wounded from both the Union and Confederate armies.

By the time the battle was over, the area had been ravaged. Fighting had occurred over twenty-five square miles.[5] Homes had been hit by shells and bullets. Fences and crops had been destroyed. Farm animals were lost.

The town's Evergreen Cemetery had been the scene of some terrible fighting. By the battle's end, it was littered with dead horses and broken guns. Many of the grave markers had been struck by bullets. Some were merely pockmarked. Others were shattered.

The Army of the Potomac Leaves

The Union Army of the Potomac left the field beginning on July 5. Union soldiers did not finish burying the dead until July 6. They continued to take the time to bury the Union dead in individual, marked graves. They threw the Confederates, on the other hand, into mass graves. Because of a lack of time, they simply left hundreds of dead horses where they had fallen. The stench would linger over the town for weeks.[6]

The last Union corps left the area on July 7. Northern militias then arrived to guard the town. They would leave by the first of August.[7]

On July 7, representatives of the United States Sanitary Commission, an organization much like today's Red Cross, arrived in Gettysburg. It started to set up hospitals and care for the wounded the Union Army had left behind. By July 23, the Sanitary Commission had established Camp Letterman, where tents served as hospitals. The last Confederate prisoners began their march to Union prisons on July 16.[8]

News of Gettysburg Spreads

News of the battle spread quickly across the United States, the Confederacy, and around the globe. Both armies had been accompanied by foreign observers, who sent messages about the battle to Europe. European leaders had never officially supported the Confederacy, but some had seemed likely to do so. They would soon decide not to send the Confederates money or soldiers to help fight the war.

Journalists from the nearby cities of Baltimore, Philadelphia, and Washington, D.C., wrote accounts for newspapers just as quickly as they could gather information. Some Northern newspapers exaggerated the extent of the Union victory. The *New York Tribune*, for example, reported on July 6 that Lee's army had suffered a total defeat. It also claimed that Union troops surrounded what little remained of Lee's army. According to the *Tribune*, Lee and the men he had left would never make it back to Virginia. They would die or be forced to surrender.[9]

On the other hand, at first some Southern newspapers did not report the extent of the Confederate defeat. It took them time to learn how badly the battle had turned out for their troops. Eventually, however, Southerners learned the truth, both from newspapers and from letters Confederate soldiers sent home.

On July 5, a team of photographers—Alexander Gardner, Timothy O'Sullivan, and James F. Gibson—arrived in Gettysburg and started to take photographs. Altogether they would take about sixty photographs. Many were of corpses and graves. Historian William Frassanito concluded that their purpose was really "to record the horrors of war rather than the area's landmarks."[10]

Famous photographer Mathew Brady arrived a few days later. Although none of his photographs included bodies, he did make numerous photographs of the places where fighting occurred. Copies of these photographs of Gettysburg were sold. Some were also copied as engravings, which appeared in the magazines of the day.

After the battle was over, soldiers sent letters describing it to their families. The Union troops rejoiced. Robert G. Carter of Massachusetts wrote to his father on July 14, 1863:

> We went into the bloody battle of Gettysburg feeling that we had suffered too much for the wretches, not to give them a *licking*, and we fought like *devils*. . . . [We] fought one of the most terrible battles on record and *whipped*—GLORY!!! *and chased them by thunder!!!!*[11]

Despite this initial enthusiasm, however, Union morale would soon fall off.

Meade Pursues Lee

President Abraham Lincoln wanted General Meade to follow Lee and force him to fight once more. Lincoln hoped Lee's army could be cut off and destroyed. But Meade never caught up with Lee. The Union Army did follow and harass Lee, but it never attacked. On the march south, following Lee, the Union soldiers were tired, dirty, hungry, and due to rain, wet.[12] The Army of the Potomac had lost many men. Three of the seven corps commanders had either died or been wounded at Gettysburg, which meant command had had to change hands.

Many histories mistakenly argue that Meade never wanted to attack Lee. On July 12, Meade's Army of the Potomac approached Lee's Army of Northern Virginia, which was then near Hagerstown, Maryland. Meade told Henry Halleck that the Union Army would attack the next day "unless something intervenes to prevent it."[13]

The next morning, however, Meade's officers persuaded him to postpone the assault. They wanted to learn more about Lee's position and strength. However, bad weather—fog and rain—prevented Union soldiers from going out to find such information. Their reconnaissance was re-scheduled for July 14.

By July 14, however, the opportunity to gather information had passed. When the Confederate Army of Northern Virginia reached the Potomac River on July 12, they found it too high to cross. Lee, however, had a makeshift bridge built. On July 13, the Confederate Army used it to slip away. On July 14, the Union Army discovered that almost all the Confederates had escaped.

Rather than attack the entire Confederate Army, the Union cavalry attacked a rearguard. Confederate Brigadier General Johnston Pettigrew, who had fought bravely at Gettysburg, was mortally wounded. Another thousand Confederate men may have also become casualties, but it is hard to be sure. Union and Confederate accounts of the engagement differed widely. Lee denied that any more than a few men died or were wounded in Maryland.[14]

At any rate, this fighting ended the Confederate Army's Gettysburg Campaign. As soon as the last Confederates crossed the bridge they had built, they cut the ropes holding it and it floated downstream. The Army of the Potomac remained behind, in Union territory.

Back in the South

Back home, Lee and his men found themselves still the object of affection and the cause of confidence among the Southern people. The South remained committed to its cause and continued to fight to defend itself from the Union armies that would continue to invade.

The North, on the other hand, had had its morale restored. The peace movement lost its momentum for a time. After the Battle of Gettysburg, the nation recommitted to fighting.

THE
GETTYSBURG
ADDRESS

In November 1863, the town of Gettysburg, Pennsylvania, made newspaper headlines for a second time. Within a month of the end of the Battle of Gettysburg, local lawyer David Wills suggested the establishment of a national Union cemetery there. His fellow townspeople liked the idea. The seventeen states that had lost citizens in the battle there all agreed.

That fall, workers began to dig up the bodies of the 3,512 Union soldiers who had been hastily buried in and around Gettysburg after the battle. They would be reburied by March 1864. Eventually, all their graves would be marked by marble headstones. One third of the dead, however, could not be identified by name.[1]

The dedication of the Union Army cemetery at Gettysburg, Pennsylvania, would take place on November 19, 1863. Two months in advance, Edward Everett received an invitation to be the main speaker at the event. In the past, Everett had been president of Harvard University, governor of Massachusetts, a United States senator, ambassador to England, and secretary of state. Now he was one of the most famous orators in the United States. President Abraham Lincoln was also invited to say a few words. David Wills, the chair of the committee that created the cemetery, wrote to ask Lincoln to come just seventeen days before the dedication.

Lincoln Writes the Gettysburg Address

Everett wrote his remarks for the cemetery dedication far in advance. Lincoln had a copy of what Everett intended to say two weeks before the ceremony. Lincoln was so busy—the Civil War was taking up almost all his time—that he began to draft his speech on White House stationery just a couple of days before he left Washington. (Histories sometimes say he wrote it on the train, while en route to Gettysburg, but this is a myth.)

An old friend of Lincoln's, Ward Hill Lamon, remembered that, before Lincoln left, the two of them were talking about what Lincoln wanted to say at the ceremony. Lincoln expressed his dissatisfaction with what he had written. He took his draft from his hat and read it to Lamon.[2]

On November 18, Lincoln and other dignitaries boarded a train for Gettysburg. It was a bad time for Lincoln to leave the nation's capital. His son Tad was sick and he was worried about him. Nevertheless, he went. He wanted very much to see Gettysburg, where so many had spilled their blood for the Union. Lincoln and his companions spent most of their time on the train telling stories. Toward the end of the trip, Lincoln retired to a little room at the back of the railroad car to work on his speech.

Lincoln's Reception in Gettysburg

When Lincoln arrived, everyone wanted to see him. Gettysburg resident Albertus McCreary felt "thrilled" when he got close enough to see the great man close up: "He seemed very tall and gaunt to me, but his face was wonderful to look upon. It was such a sad face and so full of kindly feeling that one felt at home with him at once."[3]

Lincoln spent the night at the home of David Wills. A crowd gathered around the house. A band played and a chorus of women sang for him. Once, he came to the door and acknowledged their presence. He did not speak, however.[4]

At about ten o'clock, he retired to revise his speech once more. After eleven, Lincoln went next door to the house where Secretary of State William Seward was staying. They worked on the speech together for another half hour. No one knows to what extent Seward helped Lincoln write the Gettysburg Address.[5]

The Dedication

The next morning, the ceremony took place. Observers disagreed as to just how huge a crowd gathered on Cemetery Hill. The low estimate was fifteen thousand. Looking back, Gettysburg resident Daniel Skelly remembered that, the night before the ceremony

The dedication ceremony of the memorial cemetery at Gettysburg took place in November 1863.

was held, the town's four hotels were packed. Every single house was filled to overflowing, too. Many people who could not find a bed stayed up all night, walking around town. Thousands arrived very early the morning of the ceremony.

Officials paraded to the new cemetery. Some walked. Others, like Lincoln, rode horses. Once there, the crowd waited an hour for the arrival of Edward Everett. He was late because he had decided he needed to work on his own speech just a little more. In the meantime, bands played. The audience, including Lincoln, waited patiently.

Once he showed up, Everett delivered a flowery speech filled with fancy words and references to ancient Greek warriors. He began:

Standing beneath this serene sky, overlooking these broad fields now reposing from the labors of the waning year, the mighty Alleghenies dimly towering before us, the graves of our brethren beneath our feet, it is with hesitation that I raise my poor voice to break the eloquent silence of God and Nature. . . .[6]

He went on for just minutes under two hours.

A glee club then sang. During its performance, Lincoln pulled his speech from his pocket, put on his glasses, and read through it silently. Once the choir finished, Lincoln's friend Ward Hill Lamon rose and said simply, "The President of the United States." Lincoln stood up and gave his address. He spoke loudly and clearly. Just once or twice he looked at the two sheets of paper on which the speech was written. The address of about 270 words took him less than three minutes to deliver. It went by so quickly that the photographer assigned to cover the event did not have time to adjust his camera. Thus he failed to capture the moment for posterity. Witness Daniel Skelly said, "As I remember it, [the Gettysburg Address] was received with very little, if any applause."[7] Skelly explained that the audience included many people who had lost friends and relations. The crowd as a whole did not expect the fighting to come to an end soon. They saw little to clap about.

The Significance of the Gettysburg Address

Today, the Gettysburg Address is remembered as one of the greatest speeches ever delivered. Everett recognized its importance immediately. He wrote to

FOUR SCORE AND SEVEN YEARS AGO, OUR FATHERS BROUGHT FORTH ON THIS CONTINENT, A NEW NATION, CONCEIVED IN LIBERTY, AND DEDICATED TO THE PROPOSITION THAT ALL MEN ARE CREATED EQUAL.

NOW WE ARE ENGAGED IN A GREAT CIVIL WAR, TESTING WHETHER THAT NATION OR ANY NATION SO CONCEIVED AND SO DEDICATED, CAN LONG ENDURE. WE ARE MET ON A GREAT BATTLE-FIELD OF THAT WAR. WE HAVE COME TO DEDICATE A PORTION OF THAT FIELD, AS A FINAL RESTING PLACE FOR THOSE WHO HERE GAVE THEIR LIVES THAT THAT NATION MIGHT LIVE. IT IS ALTOGETHER FITTING AND PROPER THAT WE SHOULD DO THIS.

BUT, IN A LARGER SENSE, WE CAN NOT DEDICATE—WE CAN NOT CONSECRATE—WE CAN NOT HALLOW—THIS GROUND. THE BRAVE MEN, LIVING AND DEAD, WHO STRUGGLED HERE, HAVE CONSECRATED IT FAR ABOVE OUR POOR POWER TO ADD OR DETRACT. THE WORLD WILL LITTLE NOTE, NOR LONG REMEMBER WHAT WE SAY HERE, BUT IT CAN NEVER FORGET WHAT THEY DID HERE. IT IS FOR US THE LIVING, RATHER, TO BE DEDICATED HERE TO THE UNFINISHED WORK WHICH THEY WHO FOUGHT HERE HAVE THUS FAR SO NOBLY ADVANCED. IT IS RATHER FOR US TO BE HERE DEDICATED TO THE GREAT TASK REMAINING BEFORE US—THAT FROM THESE HONORED DEAD WE TAKE INCREASED DEVOTION TO THAT CAUSE FOR WHICH THEY GAVE THE LAST FULL MEASURE OF DEVOTION—THAT WE HERE HIGHLY RESOLVE THAT THESE DEAD SHALL NOT HAVE DIED IN VAIN—THAT THIS NATION, UNDER GOD, SHALL HAVE A NEW BIRTH OF FREEDOM—AND THAT GOVERNMENT OF THE PEOPLE, BY THE PEOPLE, FOR THE PEOPLE, SHALL NOT PERISH FROM THE EARTH.[8]

Abraham Lincoln's Gettysburg Address, received with minimal acclaim at the time, has become one of the best-known speeches in American history.

Lincoln: "I would be glad if I could flatter myself that I came as near the central idea of the occasion in two hours, as you did in two minutes."[9]

Many journalists present at the occasion made no particular remark concerning the speech. The *New York Tribune*, for instance, went on and on about Everett's speech, but said only that "The dedicatory remarks were then delivered by the President."[10] The *Chicago Tribune* was the first newspaper to state in print that it was an important speech that would "live in the annals of men."[11]

Lincoln biographer Carl Sandburg may have summed up best why the speech is still considered so important and why its words continue to move people more than a century later: "His cadences sang the ancient song that where there is freedom men have fought and sacrificed for it, and that freedom is worth men's dying for."[12] The Gettysburg Address was also significant because, in it, Lincoln promised both the North and the South that, one day, they would once more be part of a great nation. He foretold a great future for the United States.

9

THE LEGACY

The defeat of the Confederate Army of Northern Virginia at the Battle of Gettysburg did not mean the end of the Confederacy. The Civil War dragged on for another two years. After Gettysburg, however, Southerners never again tried to fight the war on Union soil.

The Confederacy weakened considerably after Union General Ulysses S. Grant forced the city of Vicksburg, Mississippi, to surrender the day after the Battle of Gettysburg ended. Union control of the Mississippi River meant that the Confederate states in the West were cut off from those in the East. Nevertheless, Confederates continued to fight valiantly, defending their new country from the Union soldiers they considered invaders.

In 1864, however, their situation worsened. The Union Army took over Atlanta, Georgia. Led by General William T. Sherman, Union troops left a path of destruction behind as they marched toward Savannah. After seizing Savannah, Sherman's army marched north to Columbia, the capital of South Carolina.

Today, the battlefield at Gettysburg is a popular attraction.
Civil War battle reenactments are often held there.

SOURCE DOCUMENT

19 FEBRUARY, COLUMBIA. GENERAL SHERMAN HAS GIVEN ORDERS FOR THE FARTHER DESTRUCTION OF ALL PUBLIC PROPERTY IN THE CITY, EXCEPTING THE NEW CAPITOL, WHICH WILL NOT BE INJURED. I THINK THE GENERAL SAVES THIS BUILDING MORE BECAUSE IT IS A BEAUTIFUL WORK OF ART THAN FOR ANY OTHER REASON. THE ARSENAL, RAILROAD, DEPOTS, STOREHOUSES, MAGAZINES, PUBLIC PROPERTY, AND COTTON TO THE AMOUNT OF 20,000 BALES ARE TODAY DESTROYED. THERE IS NOT A RAIL UPON ANY OF THE ROADS WITHIN TWENTY MILES OF COLUMBIA BUT WILL BE TWISTED INTO CORKSCREWS BEFORE THE SUN SETS.[1]

George Nichols described the destructive march of General William Tecumseh Sherman's march through the cities of the South.

The End of the War

By the spring of 1865, Union soldiers had entered every state in the Confederacy except for Texas and Florida. Union General Grant fought Confederate General Lee in Virginia. By the end, the Confederacy was exhausted. Its armies were desperately short of men and supplies. Finally, General Robert E. Lee and his Confederate army became cornered. They had to surrender.

The Confederate troops laid down their arms at Appomattox Court House, Virginia, on April 9, 1865. Just days later, on April 14, another momentous event occurred. Abraham Lincoln was shot by a fanatic Confederate named John Wilkes Booth. He died the following morning. Soon Confederates stopped fighting in the West, too. Union troops then captured Confederate President Jefferson Davis in May. The Confederacy was no more.

The Gettysburg Debate

What happened at Gettysburg? Why did Lee lose? How did Meade win? These are questions that have been debated for years. They will likely still be argued more than a century from now.

Even before the war was over, participants talked a lot about the battle, placing blame and taking credit. Lee himself wrote a very short official report regarding the battle. He blamed none of his officers. In 1870, however, he and William Allan met on several occasions to discuss the war. After one of their conversations, Allan recorded that Lee had said, "Stuart failed to give him information and this deceived him into a general battle." Lee also discussed how much he had missed General Stonewall Jackson, who had died right before the Gettysburg Campaign began. Allan wrote that Lee "often thinks that if [Stonewall] Jackson had been there he would have succeeded."[2]

Other former Confederate officers accused each other of having failed to do their duty at Gettysburg. Criticism of Lee was generally very gentle, but General James Longstreet suggested that Lee had been at fault.[3] Longstreet himself also came under fire. J.E.B. Stuart was faulted for failing to guard the Army of

At Gettysburg today, many monuments stand in memory of those on both sides who fought and died there.

Northern Virginia. A. P. Hill was accused of starting the battle, and Richard Ewell was criticized for failing to seize the hills the Union took on the afternoon of the first day of the battle.

Gettysburg may be the best-known battle in American military history. It has received an enormous amount of scholarly attention. Historians in particular discuss why Lee lost. One argument stated that Lee was used to being able to count on his lieutenants. He and Jackson had worked very well together. With Jackson, Lee had seldom interfered. Lee would discuss his strategy with Jackson before battles, but once fighting broke out, Lee trusted Jackson to make his own decisions. At Gettysburg, Lee no longer had Jackson. The Army of Northern Virginia's command structure was new. Some historians have argued that Lee made a terrible mistake when he failed to exert personal control there.[4]

Historians also debate the significance of Gettysburg. Some believe this battle represented the "high tide" for the Confederacy. At its outset, the new nation had the greatest possibility of winning the Civil War. Some consider Lee's loss there to have been the "turning point" in the war. Others disagree. They argue that, even if Robert E. Lee had won at Gettysburg, he might not have been able to continue his invasion of the North. He had lost too many men and he lacked crucial supplies.[5]

Gettysburg as a Historic Site

Although controversy exists about the significance of the battle, there is no doubt about the enormous interest it holds for Americans. Interest in the battle site was high from the beginning. The national cemetery was dedicated in November 1863. In June 1864, a fair took place in Philadelphia. Women from around Gettysburg were asked to collect battlefield trophies. By that time, relatively few objects could still be found in the fields. But the women crafted items from grass and moss of the battlefield, which sold very well.[6] On July 4, 1865, President Andrew Johnson went to Gettysburg to oversee the laying of the cornerstone of a Soldiers' National Monument.[7] By that time, the town and battlefield were already tourist attractions.

Efforts to preserve the battlefield began soon after the war ended. Northerners erected many more monuments and markers, in memory of the Union soldiers who had become heroes there. Soon after the twenty-fifth anniversary of the battle in 1888, Northerners also began to talk more about the courage of the Confederates in the battle. Markers were put up to commemorate their deeds, too.

Until 1895, the battlefield was maintained by the Gettysburg Battlefield Memorial Association. At that point, the federal government acquired it and established Gettysburg National Park. In 1913, on the battle's fiftieth anniversary, for the first time, a large number of Confederates held a reunion at the park.[8]

Today, thousands of Americans visit the park every year. Walking through the museum there, across the battlefields, and through the cemetery, they often feel mixed emotions, from sorrow to horror. Leaving, they express awe at the courage both sides displayed. Utterly dedicated to their causes, soldiers from both the North and the South fought with determination and had to make supreme sacrifices at Gettysburg. The loss of life sustained there was one of the greatest tragedies in American history.

★ TIMELINE ★

1861—*April 12*: The Civil War begins when Confederate soldiers fire on Fort Sumter, South Carolina.

1861—*July*: The First Battle of Bull Run ends as a Confederate victory.

1862—*September 17*: The Battle of Antietam takes place in Maryland, on Union soil.

1863—*May 1–4*: The Battle of Chancellorsville ends with a Confederate win.
May 17: The Confederate Cabinet votes, approving Confederate General Robert E. Lee's plan to take his Army of Northern Virginia on an invasion of the North.
May 18: Union General Ulysses S. Grant begins his siege of Vicksburg, Mississippi.
June 3: The first parts of Lee's army begin their march north from Virginia, heading toward Pennsylvania; This marks the beginning of the Gettysburg Campaign.
June 9: Lee's cavalry, under the command of J.E.B. Stuart, is surprised by Union cavalry and fights the Battle of Brandy Station; The battle ends as a draw but demonstrates that the Union cavalry has learned to fight as well as the Confederate.
June 15: The Army of Northern Virginia crosses into Maryland.
June 24: The first units of Lee's army reach Pennsylvania; Lee loses contact with Stuart.

June 28: Abraham Lincoln gives George Meade command of the Army of the Potomac.

June 29: Meade joins his army near Maryland.

June 30: A small number of Confederate and Union soldiers reach Gettysburg, Pennsylvania.

July 1: The Battle of Gettysburg starts as a chance engagement; By the end of the day, the Confederates can claim victory.

July 2: The second day of the Battle of Gettysburg; The Union troops take and hold key positions, although the Confederates inflict terrible losses on them.

July 3: The third and final day of the Battle of Gettysburg; Pickett's Charge fails and the Army of Northern Virginia is forced to retreat, after suffering terrible casualties.

July 4: It seems possible that fighting will break out once more, but Meade never attacks; During the night, Lee starts to move his troops back to Virginia; Vicksburg, Mississippi, surrenders to Union General Grant.

July 14: The Army of Northern Virginia escapes across the Potomac River.

November 19: At the dedication of a cemetery for the Union dead at Gettysburg, Abraham Lincoln delivers his Gettysburg Address.

★ CHAPTER NOTES ★

Chapter 2. Background of the Battle of Gettysburg

1. Geoffrey C. Ward, Ric Burns, and Ken Burns, *The Civil War: An Illustrated History* (New York: Alfred A. Knopf, 1991), p. 34.

2. Richard Hofstadter, ed., "Abraham Lincoln, First Inaugural Address, March 4, 1861," *Great Issues in American History: From the Revolution to the Civil War, 1765–1865* (New York: Vintage Books, 1958), vol. 2, p. 391.

3. Joseph T. Glatthaar, "The Common Soldier's Gettysburg Campaign," *The Gettysburg Nobody Knows*, ed. Gabor S. Boritt (New York: Oxford University Press, 1997), p. 4.

4. Jerome B. Agel, ed., *Words That Make America Great* (New York: Random House, 1997), p. 214.

5. Glatthaar, p. 4.

6. Joseph E. Persico, *My Enemy, My Brother* (New York: Da Capo Press, 1996), p. 49.

7. Richard McMurry, "The Pennsylvania Gambit and the Gettysburg Splash," *The Gettysburg Nobody Knows*, ed. Gabor S. Boritt (New York: Oxford University Press, 1997), p. 196.

Chapter 3. The Gettysburg Campaign Begins

1. Gary W. Gallagher, "Confederate Corps Leadership on the First Day at Gettysburg: A. P. Hill and Richard S. Ewell in a Difficult Debut," *The First Day at Gettysburg*, ed. Gary W. Gallagher (Kent, Ohio: Kent State University Press, 1992), p. 31.

2. Harry W. Pfanz, "Old Jack Is Not Here," *The Gettysburg Nobody Knows*, ed. Gabor S. Boritt (New York: Oxford University Press, 1997), p. 58.

3. Geoffrey C. Ward, Ric Burns, and Ken Burns, *The Civil War: An Illustrated History* (New York: Alfred A. Knopf, 1990), p. 142.

4. Emory M. Thomas, "Eggs, Aldie, Shepherdstown, and J.E.B. Stuart," *The Gettysburg Nobody Knows*, ed. Gabor S. Boritt (New York: Oxford University Press, 1997), pp. 103–104.

5. Shelby Foote, *The Civil War: A Narrative, Fredericksburg to Meridian* (New York: Vintage Books, 1986), p. 437.

6. Thomas, p. 103.

7. Quoted in Joseph T. Glatthaar, "The Common Soldier's Gettysburg Campaign," *The Gettysburg Nobody Knows*, ed. Gabor S. Boritt (New York: Oxford University Press, 1997), p. 7.

8. Foote, p. 441.

9. Andrew Carroll, ed., "President Abraham Lincoln to General 'Fighting Joe' Hooker," *Letters of a Nation* (New York: Kodansha International, 1997), pp. 119–120.

10. Quoted in Jim Murphy, *The Long Road to Gettysburg* (New York: Clarion Books, 1992), p. 10.

11. Quoted in Glatthaar, p. 8.

12. Ibid., p. 9.

13. Ibid., p. 10.

14. Glatthaar, p. 11.

15. Quoted in Glatthaar, p. 6.

16. Quoted in Gallagher, p. 66.

17. Ibid.

18. J. Matthew Gallman with Susan Baker, "Gettysburg's Gettysburg: What the Battle Did to the Borough," *The Gettysburg Nobody Knows*, ed. Gabor S. Boritt (New York: Oxford University Press, 1997), p. 144.

19. Jim Slade and John Alexander, *Firestorm at Gettysburg: Civilian Voices, June–November 1863* (Atglen, Penn.: Schiffer Military/Aviation History, 1998), p. 17.

20. Gallman and Baker, p. 149.

21. Gallagher, p. 41.

22. U.S. War Department, *The War of the Rebellion: A Compilation of the Official Records of the Union and Confederate Armies* (Washington, D.C.: Government Printing Office, 1880–1901), series I, volume 27, part 2, p. 307.

23. Quoted in Gallagher, p. 44.

24. Quoted in Slade and Alexander, p. 19.

25. Quoted in Gallman and Baker, p. 158.

26. Slade and Alexander, p. 29.

27. Glatthaar, pp. 4, 13.

Chapter 4. The First Day: July 1, 1863

1. Edwin B. Coddington, *The Gettysburg Campaign: A Study in Command* (New York: Charles Scribner's Sons, 1968), p. 207.

2. Paul S. Boyer et al., *The Enduring Vision: A History of the American People* (Boston: D. C. Heath, 1994), vol. 2, p. 486.

3. Gary W. Gallagher, "Confederate Corps Leadership on the First Day at Gettysburg: A. P. Hill and Richard S. Ewell in a Difficult Debut," *The First Day at Gettysburg*, ed. Gary W. Gallagher (Kent, Ohio: Kent State University Press, 1992), pp. 33, 44.

4. Ibid., p. 32.

5. Jim Murphy, *The Long Road to Gettysburg* (New York: Clarion Books, 1992), p. 44.

6. Jim Slade and John Alexander, *Firestorm at Gettysburg: Civilian Voices, June–November 1863* (Atglen, Penn.: Schiffer Military/Aviation History, 1998), p. 39.

7. Ibid.

8. Ibid., p. 49.

9. Quoted in Champ Clark, *Gettysburg: The Confederate High Tide* (Alexandria, Va.: Time-Life Books, 1985), p. 35.

10. Quoted in Murphy, p. 46.

11. Shelby Foote, *The Civil War: A Narrative, Fredericksburg to Meridian* (Norwalk, Conn.: The Easton Press, 1998), p. 470.

12. Robert K. Krick, "Three Confederate Disasters on Oak Ridge: Failures of Brigade Leadership on the First Day at Gettysburg," *The First Day at Gettysburg*, ed. Gary W. Gallagher (Kent, Ohio: Kent State University Press, 1992), p. 99.

13. Slade and Alexander, p. 49.

14. Ibid., p. 53.

15. Joseph E. Persico, *My Enemy, My Brother* (New York: Da Capo Press, 1996), p. 35.

16. Krick, p. 127.

17. Ibid., p. 133.

18. Ibid., p. 134.

19. V. E. Turner and H. C. Wall, "Twenty-third Regiment," *Histories of the Several Regiments and Battalions from North Carolina in the Great War, 1861-'65*, ed. Walter Clark (Wendell, N.C.: Avera Press for Broadfoot's Bookmark, 1982), vol. 2, p. 235.

20. Slade and Alexander, p. 53.

21. Samuel Wilkinson, "Gettysburg: The Confederate Bombardment, 3 July, 1863," *Eyewitness to History*, ed. John Carey (New York: Avon Books, 1987), p. 369.

22. Foote, p. 476.

23. Slade and Alexander, pp. 63, 64.

24. A. Wilson Greene, "Howard and Eleventh Corps Leadership," *The First Day at Gettysburg*, ed. Gary W. Gallagher (Kent, Ohio: Kent State University Press, 1992), p. 83.

25. Slade and Alexander, p. 64.

26. William A. Frassanito, *Gettysburg: A Journey in Time* (New York: Charles Scribner's Sons, 1975), p. 76.

27. Quoted in Gallagher, p. 46.

28. Harry W. Pfanz, "Old Jack Is Not Here," *The Gettysburg Nobody Knows*, ed. Gabor S. Boritt (New York: Oxford University Press, 1997), p. 64.

29. Quoted in Gallagher, p. 34.

30. Ibid., p. 35.

31. Ibid., p. 36.

32. Ibid., p. 40.

Chapter 5. The Second Day: July 2, 1863

1. Robert K. Krick, "'If Longstreet . . . Says So, It is Most Likely Not True': James Longstreet and the Second Day at Gettysburg," *The Second Day at Gettysburg: Essays on Confederate and Union Leadership*, ed. Gary W. Gallagher (Kent, Ohio: Kent State University Press, 1993), p. 69.

2. Quoted in Krick, p. 74.

3. Krick, p. 69.

4. Bruce Catton, *Gettysburg: The Final Fury* (New York: Doubleday & Company, Inc., 1974), p. 38.

5. Quoted in Champ Clark, *Gettysburg: The Confederate High Tide* (Alexandria, Va.: Time-Life Books, 1985), p. 79.

6. Clark, p. 83.

7. Ibid., p. 68.

8. Geoffrey C. Ward, Ric Burns, and Ken Burns, *The Civil War: An Illustrated History* (New York: Alfred A. Knopf, 1990), p. 225.

9. Joseph T. Glatthaar, "The Common Soldier's Gettysburg Campaign," *The Gettysburg Nobody Knows*, ed. Gabor S. Boritt (New York: Oxford University Press, 1997), p. 20.

10. Ibid., p. 20.

11. Jim Slade and John Alexander, *Firestorm at Gettysburg: Civilian Voices, June–November 1863* (Atglen, Penn.: Schiffer Military/Aviation History, 1998), pp. 88, 89.

12. Ibid., p. 102.

13. Ibid., pp. 89, 91, 92.

14. Clark, p. 71.

15. Emory M. Thomas, "Eggs, Aldie, Shepherdstown, and J.E.B. Stuart," *The Gettysburg Nobody Knows*, ed. Gabor S. Boritt (New York: Oxford University Press, 1997), p. 107.

16. Quoted in Jim Murphy, *The Long Road to Gettysburg* (New York: Clarion Books, 1992), p. 65.

Chapter 6. The Third Day: July 3, 1863

1. Joseph E. Persico, *My Enemy, My Brother* (New York: Da Capo Press, 1996), p. 195.

2. David Colbert, ed., "Gettysburg," *Eyewitness to America: 500 Years of America in the Words of Those Who Saw It Happen* (New York: Pantheon Books, 1997), p. 226.

3. Champ Clark, *Gettysburg: The Confederate High Tide* (Alexandria, Va.: Time-Life Books, 1985), p. 132.

4. Ibid.

5. Douglas Southall Freeman, *Lee's Lieutenants* (New York: Charles Scribner's Sons, 1942–1944), vol. 2, p. 659.

6. William A. Frassanito, *Gettysburg: A Journey in Time* (New York: Charles Scribner's Sons, 1975), p. 95.

7. Carol Reardon, "I Think the Union Army Had Something to Do With It: The Pickett's Charge Nobody Knows," *The Gettysburg Nobody Knows*, ed. Gabor S. Boritt (New York: Oxford University Press, 1997), p. 125.

8. Joseph T. Glatthaar, "The Common Soldier's Gettysburg Campaign," *The Gettysburg Nobody Knows*, ed. Gabor S. Borritt (New York: Oxford University Press, 1997), p. 25.

9. Piston, p. 45.

10. Reardon, p. 127.

11. Clark, p. 136.

12. Quoted in Clark, p. 137.

13. Reardon, p. 132.

14. Quoted in Clark, p. 138.

15. Geoffrey C. Ward, Ric Burns, and Ken Burns, *The Civil War: An Illustrated History* (New York: Alfred A. Knopf, 1990), p. 235.

16. Quoted in Clark, p. 145.

17. Jim Slade and John Alexander, *Firestorm at Gettysburg: Civilian Voices, June–November 1863* (Atglen, Penn.: Schiffer Military/Aviation History, 1998), p. 126.

18. Ibid., p. 128.

19. Ibid., p. 130.

Chapter 7. Aftermath

1. Shelby Foote, *The Civil War: A Narrative, Fredericksburg to Meridian* (New York: Vintage Books, 1986), p. 587.

2. Douglas Southall Freeman, *Lee's Lieutenants* (New York: Charles Scribner's Sons, 1942–1944), vol. 2, p. 190.

3. J. Matthew Gallman with Susan Baker, "Gettysburg's Gettysburg: What the Battle Did to the Borough," *The Gettysburg Nobody Knows*, ed. Gabor S. Boritt (New York: Oxford University Press, 1997), pp. 148, 160.

4. Ibid., p. 145.

5. William A. Frassanito, *Gettysburg: A Journey in Time* (New York: Charles Scribner's Sons, 1975), p. 59.

6. Jim Slade and John Alexander, *Firestorm at Gettysburg: Civilian Voices, June–November 1863* (Atglen, Penn.: Schiffer Military/Aviation History, 1998), p. 7.

7. Frassanito, pp. 55, 112.

8. Ibid., p. 37.

9. A. Wilson Greene, "Meade's Pursuit of Lee: From Gettysburg to Falling Waters," *The Third Day at Gettysburg and Beyond*, ed. Gary W. Gallagher (Chapel Hill: University of North Carolina Press, 1994), p. 179.

10. Frassanito, p. 27.

11. Quoted in Gary W. Gallagher, *The Third Day at Gettysburg and Beyond* (Chapel Hill: The University of North Carolina Press, 1994), p. viii.

12. Greene, p. 168.

13. Quoted in Greene, p. 171.

14. Greene, p. 173.

Chapter 8. The Gettysburg Address

1. William A. Frassanito, *Gettysburg: A Journey in Time* (New York: Charles Scribner's Sons, 1975), p. 119.

2. Carl Sandburg, *Abraham Lincoln: The War Years* (New York: Harcourt, Brace & Company, 1938), vol. 2, p. 455.

3. Jim Slade and John Alexander, *Firestorm at Gettysburg: Civil Voices, June–November 1863* (Atglen, Penn.: Schiffer Military/Aviation History, 1998), p. 171.

4. Ibid.

5. Sandburg, p. 465.

6. Quoted in Jim Murphy, *The Long Road to Gettysburg* (New York: Clarion Books, 1992), p. 5.

7. Slade and Alexander, p. 175.

8. Abraham Lincoln, "The Gettysburg Address," November 19, 1863.

9. Sandburg, p. 475.

10. Ibid., p. 472.

11. Ibid., p. 473.

12. Ibid., p. 476.

Chapter 9. The Legacy

1. George Nichols, "The Great March: General Sherman Lays Waste to the South, October 1864–February 1865," *Eyewitness to History*, ed. John Carey (New York: Avon Books, 1987), p. 370.

2. Robert K. Krick, "Three Confederate Disasters on Oak Ridge: Failures of Brigade Leadership on the First Day at Gettysburg," *The First Day at Gettysburg*, ed. Gary W. Gallagher (Kent, Ohio: Kent State University Press, 1992), p. 139.

3. Gary W. Gallagher, *The Third Day at Gettysburg and Beyond* (Chapel Hill: The University of North Carolina Press, 1994), p. 30.

4. Quoted in Gallagher, p. 93.

5. Richard McMurry, "The Pennsylvania Gambit and the Gettysburg Splash," *The Gettysburg Nobody Knows*, ed. Gabor S. Boritt (New York: Oxford University Press, 1997), pp. 201–202.

6. J. Matthew Gallman with Susan Baker, "Gettysburg's Gettysburg: What the Battle Did to the Borough," *The Gettysburg Nobody Knows*, ed. Gabor S. Boritt (New York: Oxford University Press, 1997), p. 164.

7. Ibid., p. 173.

8. Amy J. Kinsel, "Gettysburg National Park," *The Third Day at Gettysburg and Beyond*, ed. Gary W. Gallagher (Chapel Hill: The University of North Carolina Press, 1994), p. 208.

★ FURTHER READING ★

Books

Boritt, Gabor S., ed. *The Gettysburg Nobody Knows*. New York: Oxford University Press, 1997.

Clark, Champ. *Gettysburg: The Confederate High Tide*. Alexandria, Va.: Time-Life Books, 1985.

Corrick, James A. *The Battle of Gettysburg: Battles of the Civil War*. San Diego, Calif.: Lucent Books, 1996.

Kent, Zachary. *The Civil War: "A House Divided."* Hillside, N.J.: Enslow Publishers, Inc., 1994.

Kerby, Mona. *Robert E. Lee: Southern Hero of the Civil War*. Springfield, N.J.: Enslow Publishers, Inc., 1997.

Murphy, Jim. *The Long Road to Gettysburg*. New York: Houghton Mifflin Company, 1992.

Pflueger, Lynda. *Jeb Stuart: Confederate Cavalry General*. Springfield, N.J.: Enslow Publishers, Inc., 1998.

Internet Addresses

Library of Congress. *The Gettysburg Address*. May 17, 1999. <http://lcweb.loc.gov/exhibits/gadd/>.

National Park Service. *Gettysburg National Military Park*. June 2, 2000. <http://www.nps.gov/gett/index.htm>.

★ INDEX ★

A
abolition movement, 10
Alexander, E. Porter, 84
Allan, William, 109
Archer, James J., 46, 48, 52
Armistead, Lewis, 86–87
Army of Northern Virginia, 6, 7,
   8, 14–15, 16, 19, 21, 24, 26,
   31–33, 36, 42, 54, 59, 60,
   61, 62, 77, 90, 91–92, 97,
   106, 109–111
Army of the Potomac, 18, 19, 23,
   27, 35–36, 40, 42, 59, 60,
   71, 75, 94, 97, 98

B
Baltimore, Maryland, 25, 36, 95
Battle of Antietam, 15–16, 17
Battle of Chancellorsville, 18–19,
   23, 24, 35
Battle of Gettysburg,
   campaign, 23, 23, 25, 26, 27,
     29, 30–36
   cemetery, 94, 99–105
   chance encounter, 9, 42, 43
   civilians, 41–42, 45–46,
     48–49, 50–52, 55, 56, 70,
     71, 80–81, 89, 92, 93
   Confederate retreat, 89, 90,
     91, 97, 98
   dead buried, 94
   eve of, 42
   July 1 (first day), 43, 45–49,
     50–54, 55, 56–59
   July 2 (second day), 60–61,
     62, 63–64, 65–69, 70,
     71–72, 73–74
   July 3 (third day), 75–77,
     79–82, 83, 84–89
   losses, 55, 67, 68–69, 79, 88,
     91–92
   news spreads, 95, 96

Pickett's Charge, 82, 83,
   84–89
shoes (disputed role in starting
   battle), 37–38, 40
strategy, 54, 57–58, 60-61, 71,
   75
Union pursuit of
   Confederates, 96–97
why Confederates lost,
   109–111
Battle of Sharpsburg. *See* Battle
   of Antietam.
Baxter, Henry, 52
Bayly, Harriet, 46, 71
Booth, John Wilkes, 108–109
Brady, Mathew, 96
Bragg, Braxton, 15
Broadhead, Sarah, 70, 89, 93
Buford, John, 27, 29, 36, 39, 40,
   42, 46–47
Burnside, Ambrose, 16
Burns, John, 50–52
Bushman, Sadie, 49

C
Carter, Robert G., 96
Chamberlain, Joshua, 65–66
Civil War,
   Antietam, 15–16, 17
   begins, 11–13
   Brandy Station, 26, 27, 29, 30
   causes, 10–11
   Chancellorville, 18–19, 23, 24
   end, 108–109
   First Battle of Bull Run, 14, 44
   Fort Sumter, 11–13, 14
   Fredericksburg, 16, 23
   Second Bull Run, 15
   Seven Days', 15
   significance of Battle of
     Gettysburg, 106, 111
   soldiers' lives, 44–45, 73–74